Leathercraft

Linda Sue Eastman

Fox
Chapel Publishing
1970 Broad Street • East Petersburg, PA 17520
www.FoxChapelPublishing.com

ISBN 978-1-56523-370-6

Publisher's Cataloging-in-Publication Data

Eastman, Linda Sue.
    Leathercraft / Linda Sue Eastman. -- 1st ed. -- East Petersburg, PA :
Fox Chapel Publishing, c2008.

        p. ; cm.
        (Kidcrafts)

        ISBN: 978-1-56523-370-6
        Summary: Teaches the skills and techniques of working with
    leather. Includes easy-to-follow photographs and step-by-step
    instructions especially designed for kids to make 11 great projects.

        1. Leatherwork--Juvenile literature. 2. [Leatherwork.
    3. Handicraft.] I. Title. II. Series.

TT290 .E27 2008
745.53/1--dc22   2008

To learn more about the other great books from Fox Chapel Publishing, or to find a retailer
near you, call toll free 800-457-9112 or visit us at *www.FoxChapelPublishing.com*.

Note to Authors: We are always looking for talented authors to write new books in our area
of woodworking, design, and related crafts. Please send a brief letter describing your idea to
Acquisition Editor, Fox Chapel Publishing, 1970 Broad Street, East Petersburg, PA 17520.

Printed in China
10 9 8 7 6 5 4 3 2 1

Table of Contents

INTRODUCTION: How to Use This Book **4**

CHAPTER 1: All About Leather **6**

CHAPTER 2: Leatherworking Supplies **20**

CHAPTER 3: Leatherworking Tools **36**

CHAPTER 4: Projects **62**

INTRODUCTION
How to Use This Book

Good Day! Thank you for joining in the craft of leatherworking. This book is designed to guide you on an enjoyable learning journey. First, you will learn about leather, then the skills and techniques of working leather. You will use tools that are designed for leatherworking. The most exciting part of this journey is when you start building the projects. There are 11 projects in all, with suggestions to spark your imagination for more projects of your own design.

The skills you will learn in this book include:

■ how to choose leather;

■ reading drawings and making patterns;

■ cutting leather;

■ punching holes;

■ tooling leather;

■ setting rivets and snaps;

■ dyeing leather;

■ joining leather with glue and lace; and

■ finishing with oil and sealers.

Each project accents a different skill. If you tackle them in order, you will build your skills to be a successful leatherworker.

Each project has:

■ a list of tools;

■ drawings for cutting the leather parts;

■ a list of skills you will learn to use;

■ a list of materials and supplies; and

■ step-by-step instructions with photos.

At the end of the book, there is a list of resources for finding more information, tools, supplies, and leather.

Leather is an extremely versatile craft material, and the skills of working with it are practical, useful, and fun. I hope you enjoy this introductory journey into the world of leatherworking.

—Linda Sue Eastman, Winona, Minnesota

Deacon Sandel and Samuel Niewald appear as models in this book.

Linda Sue Eastman

Samuel Niewald

Deacon Sandel

Note to Adults

This book of kid-tested leatherworking projects and techniques has been designed to entice, instruct, and entertain children ages 9 to 12. The projects offer a sequential set of basic leatherworking skills that children can learn without getting ahead of their neuromuscular development. These skills empower kids to build a variety of leatherworking items, including gifts and toys they can actually use.

Every project uses simple hand tools. The discussion on supplies and tools (Chapters 2 and 3) includes step-by-step demonstrations with practice exercises. These skills are used throughout the book.

Acquiring leatherworking skills will enrich kids' lives, increase their self-confidence and develop a savvy, can-do attitude toward problem solving.

Parents can work together with their children, but group leaders and teachers should complete each project before introducing it to kids. If a group works on the project, kids can double and triple up on sets of tools. Leaders with a large group and a shortage of equipment might consider setting up workstations for each operation and cycling the kids through the stations.

Finally, remember that the best approach in teaching children is to first demonstrate a task and then supervise as they attempt it themselves. Let them try new things and make their own mistakes; they can always cut another piece of leather. Keep leatherworking a fun and enjoyable experience.

CHAPTER 1

All About Leather

Leather comes from animals

We use leather to make shoes and coats, belts and bags, car seats and sofas, and baseball gloves and footballs. It is a very flexible and versatile material, useful for many different things. That's because leather can have many different qualities, depending on how it is finished. It can be soft and supple like cloth, or stiff and tough like wood.
It can be smooth like a leather jacket, or hairy like a fur coat. It can be brown or any color of the rainbow, dull, or as shiny as a polished shoe.

Leather is made from the outer skins, or "hides," of animals. Most animal hides can be made into leather. The most common leathers come from farm animals such as cows, pigs, and sheep. Because so many animals are raised for their meat for people to eat, lots of hides are available for leather. The raw hides go from meat processing plants to tanneries for finishing into leather.

Some leathers come from the farm-raised cousins of wild animals, such as deer, ostrich, elk, buffalo, crocodile, alligator, and kangaroo. These leathers are fun and interesting to use. However, some exotic leathers such as stingray, bullfrog, shark, lizard, fish, elephant, and snake come from wild animals. These animals are not farmed, but are hunted in the wild, and some of them are endangered species. To help protect the wild animals, it is best not to use the exotic leathers.

Vegetable-tanned leathers are naturally light brown in color. Some are dyed colors at the tannery (top right). They can be tooled and stamped, dyed, and formed into shapes.

Play Ball!

Baseball gloves are made from cow leather. Major league baseballs are covered with two pieces of cow leather stitched together. You can see the stitching on the outside of the ball. At one time baseballs were made of horse hide. Little League baseballs are covered with a composite material manufactured from leather scraps.

Footballs and soccer balls are stitched together from small pieces of cow leather, though at one time they were made from pig skin. The covers are stitched inside-out, so you can't see the stitching on the outside.

Which side?

The smooth side of a piece of leather was on the outside of the animal. It is the side that had the hair or fur on it. It is called the grain side, or top grain. The other side of the leather, which is not smooth, is called the underside or the flesh side.

Leather from cows and other large animals is quite thick. It can be divided into thinner pieces of leather, called splits. The strongest split is the top grain. The inner splits are not as strong.

The flesh side of this hair-on cowhide is white and rough.

The smooth side of the leather has had the hair removed. The flesh side is the rough side.

Different Types of Common Leather

Leather Chart			
Leather	**Characteristics**	**Workability**	**Uses**
Vegetable-tanned cowhide	very durable, the only leather tanned for tooling and carving	easy to hard to work depending on weight (thickness)	bags, belts, holsters, dog collars, horse tack
Chrome-tanned cowhide	durable, light to medium weight, available in many colors and finishes	easy to work	used for all types of leather work (except tooling) because of its versatility
Hair-on cowhide	durable, comes in the colors of cows in the fields and also dyed to look like zebra, tiger and leopard	medium to work because of its hair and weight	rugs, decorative trim
Cow Suede	durable, brushed to a coarse velvet feel	easy to medium to work	chaps, fringe, moccasins, pouches. clothing
Pig and Lamb suede	very soft, form fitting, and lightweight, brushed to a soft velvety feel	easy to work	clothing, linings, trim
Sheep Shearling	soft thick wool on soft, flexible leather	tricky to work because of long hair	clothing, rugs, seats, lining, decorative accents
Deerskin	very soft and stretchy, beautiful color and feel on both sides of hide	easy to work	clothing, moccasins, small (personal) leather items, craft

Cow Leather

The most commonly used leather is the hide of the cow. That is because a great many cowhides are left over from preparing the cow's meat to eat. Think of all those steaks, hamburgers, and hot dogs! Cow leather is very versatile. It can be made into many different thickness, colors, finishes, textures, and strengths. Cowhides are large enough for big projects like furniture and long coats. One hide can be made into many, many small items. Most of what you will find at a leather shop is cowhide.

Pig and Sheep Leather

Pig hides are often made into suede, which has a fuzzy texture on both sides. The leather is soft and very nice to feel. Pigs are smaller than cows but their hides are still pretty big.

Sheep hides can be made into two very different leathers. The suede made from sheep is fine and soft. The hides can also be tanned with their wool left on. This is called sheep shearling. The hair can be trimmed short to just a half-inch long, left wild and wooly as it was on the animal, or any length in between. Have you ever snuggled your feet into slippers lined with sheep shearling? It feels fantastic!

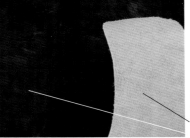

Here are both sides of a cowhide.
Flesh Side
Grain Side

Pig suede (above) and lamb suede (left) are very soft and supple. They can be dyed with bright colors, for making into clothing.

Sheep leather with the wool left on is called "shearling." This shearling has been dyed orange.

All About Leather

Bison and Deer

Leather shops sometimes have the hides of buffalo (bison), deer, and goats. These are fine leathers. Bison is particularly tough and good for shoes, and deer is quite strong while remaining soft and supple, so it's nice for clothing.

Ostrich leather

Ostrich hide looks unusual because it has bumps with pinholes in them where the feathers have been. The hides from ostrich legs are also made into leather that has the unique look and feel of scales. Most ostriches are farm raised and are used not only for their leather for clothing and upholstery but also for their eggs (to eat and to carve the shells), feathers, and meat. Real ostrich leather is very expensive, but cowhide that is textured to look and feel like ostrich is affordable.

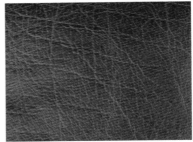

Bison leather is tough and strong.

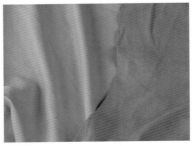

Deer leather is soft and supple.

Ostrich leather has dimples where the feathers grew.

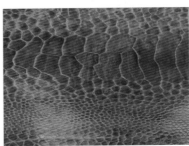

Ostrich leg has beautiful scale patterns.

Snakeskin

Western diamondhead rattlesnake is beautifully patterned and textured. The leather is thin so for strength it must be backed by another leather. These poisonous rattlesnakes were first hunted for the safety of farmers and ranchers. Today they are hunted for their meat and leather, but wisely, to maintain their population in the wild. The largest rattlesnake roundup is held every March in Sweetwater, Texas. Since the first roundup in 1958, more than 140 tons of rattlesnakes have been collected. Wow!

It is an old story that you can tell how old a rattler is by counting the number of rattles on its tail. It is only a story. The dry sections on the tail show how many times the snake has shed its skin and that can happen several times every year. Some tail sections fall off as the snake wiggles about, too. So counting the rattle sections for the snake's age is inaccurate.

Alligator and Crocodile

Aligators are farm raised in Florida, mostly for their leather. Crocodiles are farm raised in Africa for their leather and meat. A large farm can have as many as 10,000 animals on it. The crocs average nine feet long but can grow up to eighteen feet long. Can you imagine seeing one that big? Alligators are not that large. Most are harvested when they are between 6 and 7 feet long. The hides of crocodiles and alligators are coarse and bumpy. In fact, the crocodile's name comes from the Greek language, and means "pebble worm." Crocodile and alligator hides are used for dressy shoes and bags.

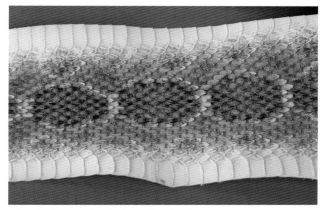

This snakeskin came from a diamondhead rattler.

Elephant Hide

African elephants are protected animals, just like the American bald eagle, so they cannot be hunted for sport. They are protected because too many were hunted for their ivory tusks. There was great worry they might become extinct. Animal reserve parks have protected the remaining animals and now the herds are growing in number. Their hides are taken when an animal has to be destroyed because it has threatened crops or injured people in nearby villages. So elephant leather is rarely available and is very expensive.

Have you ever looked at the elephants at the zoo? Their skin is very tough and rough, their hair is like wire. And their feet are gigantic!

Tanning Leather

If you left a raw animal hide out in the sun to dry, it would set hard and stiff. Tanning is a chemical process that changes the raw hides into dry, flexible leather. Hides are tanned in large, warm vats. The process is smelly and messy. There are two basic types of tanning: vegetable and chrome. Each type has advantages and disadvantages, depending on what you want to make.

Vegetable tanning uses tannic acid from tree bark, leaves, and nuts. The process leaves the leather dry and flexible, but when dampened it can be molded into shapes and carved with patterns that remain when the leather dries again. Riding saddles are made from vegetable-tanned leather that has been shaped and tooled, or stamped with patterns and designs (page 60).

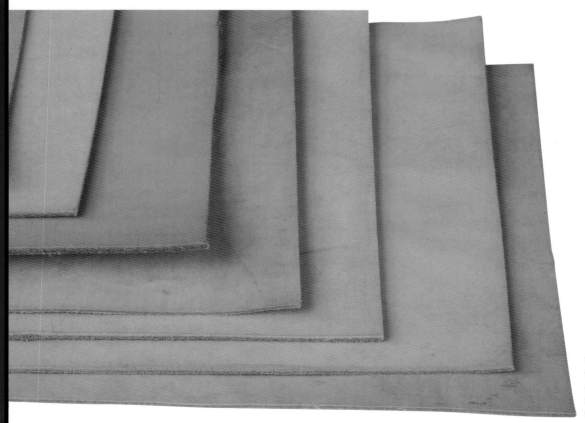

Vegetable-tanned leather is tan colored and quite stiff. It can be tooled, softened, and shaped with water, and is easy to dye another color.

Chrome tanning uses metal chromium salts to change the raw hides into usable leather. Chrome-tanned leather is very soft and flexible when dried, but it cannot be wet molded or tooled. It is usually colored and has a finish put on it at the tannery, so what you buy is complete and ready for use with no additional treatment. Leather car seats and furniture are made from chrome-tanned leather.

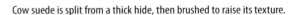

Cow suede is split from a thick hide, then brushed to raise its texture.

Suede

Suede is a soft, velvety leather finish we often see in clothing, gloves, and moccasins. Suede leather has been brushed to raise its texture. Suede from cows is split leather cut from the underside of the hide, where the fibers are loose and easy to brush. Cow split suede is very durable, which is why moccasins, cowboy chaps, and work gloves are made from it. Leather from pigs and lambs is thin, so the top grain, the outer side of the hide, is brushed to create the suede. Pig and lamb suede is known for its beautiful look and feel; it is used for decoration and fashion clothing.

Chrome-tanned leather is soft and supple. It's dyed millions of colors at the tannery. It can't be tooled.

Parts of the Hide

Most full cowhides are cut in half down the back to make two sides of leather. The back edge of the side, called the bend, is the thickest and firmest part of the side and has the fewest blemishes (or beauty marks!). Use it when you want durability with little stretch in your project, a belt for example. The middle and the neck are more bendable and flexible. This area can be used for any type of project depending on the weight you choose. Then as you move down toward the belly, the leather becomes softer and can be quite loose and stretchy. The belly is nice for small items and because it is the least expensive part of the hide it is good leather to use for practice work.

This hide came from a small-sized cow.

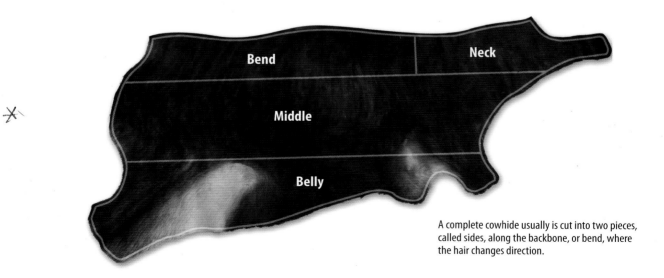

Bend

Neck

Middle

Belly

A complete cowhide usually is cut into two pieces, called sides, along the backbone, or bend, where the hair changes direction.

Leather Weight and Thickness

The main thing you'll want to know about cow leather is its thickness, but it is sold by weight per square foot. Weight and thickness actually amount to the same thing: each ounce of leather weight equals $1/64$ inch in thickness, per square foot. Tanneries try very hard to make each piece of leather uniform in thickness and weight, but some variation always will happen. So when you look for leather you will see it marked by two numbers telling you the lighter and heavier weight, such as 6/7 oz. This means a square foot of the leather will weigh between 6 and 7 ounces, so it will be at least $6/64$ (or $3/32$) inch thick, but no more than $7/64$ inch thick.

Leather Weight and Thickness Chart		
Weight per Sq. Ft.		**Thickness**
2 oz.		$1/32$"
3 oz.		$3/64$"
4 oz.		$1/16$"
5 oz.		$5/64$"
6 oz.		$3/32$"
7 oz.		$7/64$"
8 oz.		$1/8$"
9 oz.		$9/64$"
10 oz.		$5/32$"

How Much Leather to Buy?

The biggest piece of leather you can buy is a side, averaging 22 to 25 square feet. That is a lot of leather. You also can purchase smaller leather pieces in sizes from which you can make a few projects. Leather stores sell bags of scrap leather that are just smaller pieces of good leather left over from larger projects. Some of the scraps will be enough for many of the projects in this book, and they are excellent for practicing techniques.

Deciding how much leather to buy can be tricky because animal hides come in animal sizes and shapes. A cow side looks like the outline of the United States, a snake or ostrich leg hide is long and skinny.

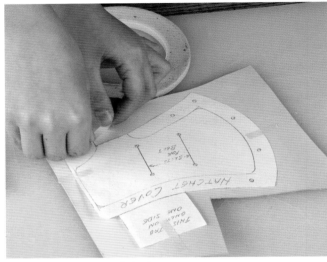

Fit your pattern pieces onto the leather.

To know how much leather to buy, you need to look at the size of your project's parts and compare them to the shape of the leather. A hide costs less per square foot but it is very big and you will have more scrap because of its odd shape. Pieces already cut from hides may cost more per square foot but you will have less scrap, so they may be the better deal. The rule of thumb is to figure the area you need and then add on 15 percent for waste scraps. Each project in this book will guide you on how much leather to buy, of what type and weight. If you can, it is best to compare your pattern parts to the leather before you buy it.

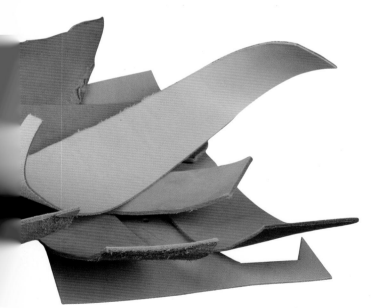

Kids can make many small projects from leather scraps such as these.

Marks and Brands

Because leather comes from nature it has its own beautiful markings. There are stretch marks, wrinkles, color variations, and fat wrinkles from the growth and movement of the animal. Some markings happen to the animal's hide during its life, such as insect bites, scratches, and brand marks. The variations in markings and textures give each piece of leather unique character. The markings do not affect the use of the leather. You can include them in the design of your project. Most people consider markings part of the beauty of the material–they are what makes leather so interesting.

The top two photos are from a vegetable-tanned cowhide that has not been colored or had a finish applied. This is how the leather will look when you buy it.

The fat wrinkles are from where the animal is heavy and has fat deposits that pull on the hide. Just as our skin has variations so does animal leather have small color changes that can be beautiful.

Ranchers brand their cattle because they roam land with cattle belonging to other ranchers. At roundup time, the ranchers can tell by the brands who owns each cow.

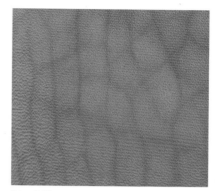

Fat wrinkles

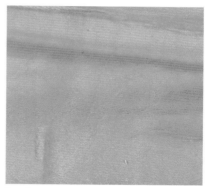

Discoloration

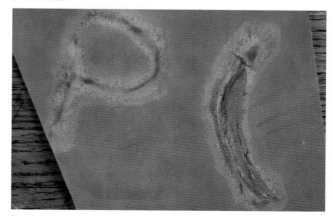

Brand marks

Choosing Leather

When selecting your leather you need to decide what qualities you want for the project you are making. Think about how your project will be used and who will use it. Pick your leather for how strong it will be–thick leather is strong and firm, but it's also difficult to cut and sew. Thin leather is flexible and easy to sew, but might not be strong or firm enough for your project. Decide if you will want to tool or carve the leather, because to do so, you will need vegetable-tanned leather. Know if your project will be used outside or indoors because that will determine what kind of finish you apply. A finish for outdoors should be waterproof and weatherproof. A finish for clothing should be nice to feel and comfortable to wear. Upholstery leather should be water resistant and comfortable to sit on. Sometimes the best finish is no finish at all, like the wallet project on page 108.

A leather-working shop has many kinds of leather in sides and rolls, stored on shelves like this.

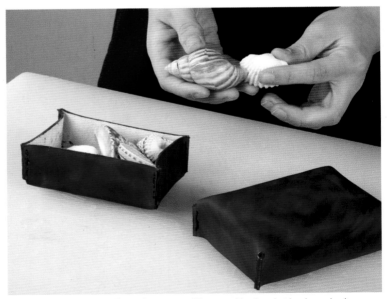

The box, page 84, is made from 4/5 oz. vegetable-tanned leather that has been dyed green.

This tooled wallet, page 108, is made from lightweight 2/3 oz. vegetable-tanned leather.

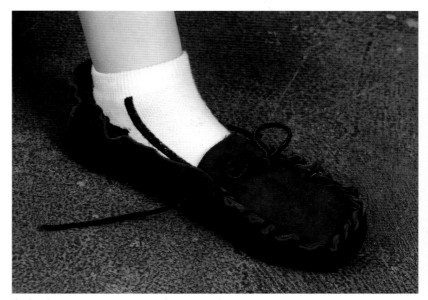

This laced moccasin, page 93, is made from cow suede.

CHAPTER 2

Leatherworking Supplies

Leatherworkers use such supplies as glue, thread, laces, dye, wax, and leather finishes. The supplies are not expensive, and small leather projects use small amounts.

The supplies shown here are what you will need for the projects in this book. Not all are needed for every project, so look at each project's supply list when you are planning to make it.

You can collect some supplies from around your house. Clean and re-use empty plastic food containers from the kitchen. For rags, old T-shirts and gym socks are great because they are absorbent and soft. Rags from old blue jeans have just the right firmness to polish leather edges. Plastic shopping bags are great to spread under messy dying and gluing jobs.

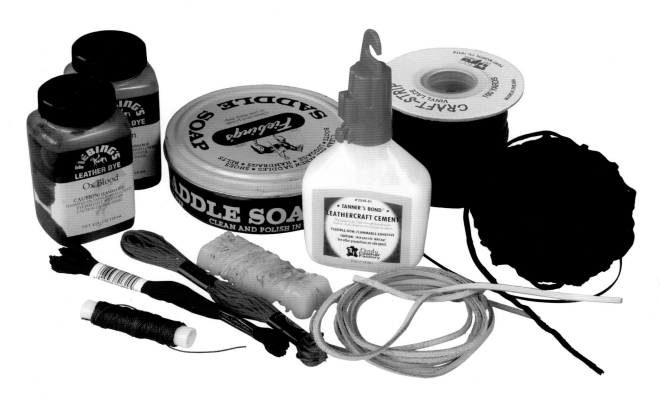

Gluing

Two different glues are commonly used in leather working. What is special about both leather glues is, they stay flexible after drying. That is important, because flexible glue will bend and not crack when your leather bends.

Glue alone is not strong enough to make a seam in leather. You can glue seams together to hold them until you sew, lace, or rivet the seam for strength. Glue alone has good strength when you are gluing two large surfaces together, for a lined book cover project or for the back of a mousepad.

The two different glues are:

■ **water-based flexible glue,** and

■ **contact cement.**

Water-based flexible glue can be bought at leather working suppliers or fabric and craft stores. The glue looks white when it is wet, so nice because you can see where it is (even the misplaced drips!) but then it dries clear. For this book's projects, flexible glue is the best glue to use because it has good strength, is easy to clean up, and is user friendly.

You could use contact cement where the glue joint needs great strength and also needs to be waterproof. Brush it onto both surfaces to be glued, then leave it alone to dry before you put the pieces together. Contact cement is a chemical glue with a strong odor and must be used outdoors or in a well-ventilated area. It is best reserved for special uses.

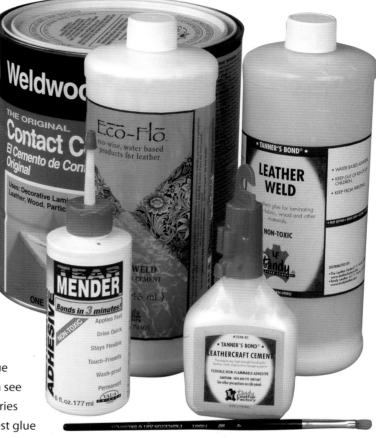

The large container in the background is contact cement. The other bottles contain flexible, water-based glues. They can be spread with a small brush.

Skills: Gluing Leather Together

1

Squeeze the Glue
Squeeze a bead of white leather glue onto one surface of the leather. Squeeze the glue all around the area you want to join.

2

Spread the Glue
Use your fingertip or a small brush to spread the glue. Cover all of the space you want to stick together. It's easy to see where the white glue is.

Flex glue works by sticking the fuzzy leather fibers together, but it will not stick well on smooth surfaces. If a glue dab dries on your fingers you can just peel it off like a little bit of rubber. Flex glue dries quickly so you can gently work with your piece again in about fifteen minutes.

Prepare your workspace by moving extra tools and leather to the side and wiping clean your work surface. Lay down a piece of plastic to protect your worktable–an old shopping bag will do. Then put your glue, brush, and leather within easy reach. Have a damp sponge ready to clean up spills.

3

Press the Glue-Up
Put the two pieces of leather together.

4

Weight the Seam
When you are gluing large areas together, use a stack of old magazines to press the leather until it dries.

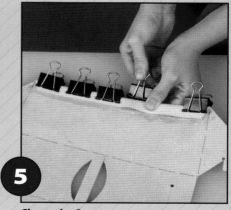

5

Clamp the Seam
To hold glued seams together while they dry you can use binder clips as clamps– they provide all the pressure you need.

Sewing and Lacing

After gluing leather seams together, it is best to sew, lace, or rivet them for strength. Sewing and lacing have very different looks. Sewing has a neat, uniform look that is nice for smaller items, while lacing looks rugged and is great for things such as the suede moccasins. There are different kinds of needles for sewing and lacing. Whether you are sewing or lacing, the first step is punching holes in the leather for the needle to pass through (page 46).

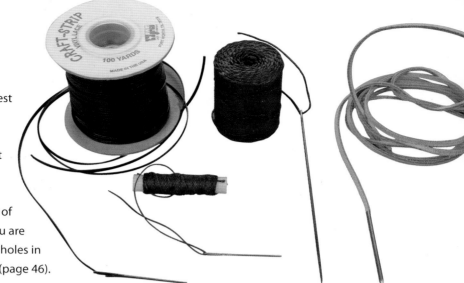

Plastic lace, top left, is flat and smooth. Leather laces, right, are thick and rough. Waxed sewing threads, center, comes in small and large spools. Each kind of thread and lace requires its own kind of needle.

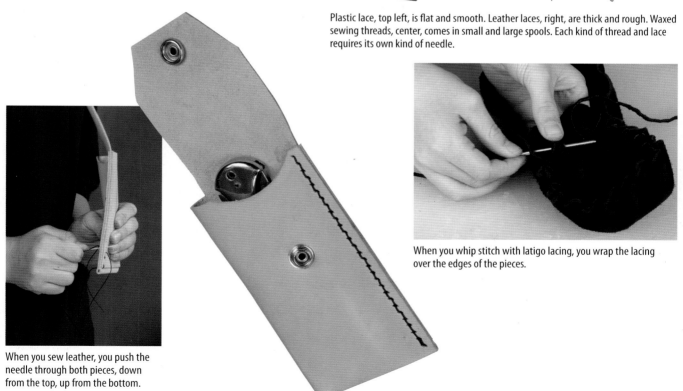

When you whip stitch with latigo lacing, you wrap the lacing over the edges of the pieces.

When you sew leather, you push the needle through both pieces, down from the top, up from the bottom.

Needles and Thread for Sewing

For sewing with thread, we use hand-stitching needles. They have an extra large eye so they are easy to thread with heavy leather-working threads. They have a blunt point to help guide the needle into punched sewing holes.

For sewing it is best to use waxed thread. The wax helps the thread to stay smooth and slide through the sewing holes. The wax also protects the thread from wear and moisture. You can buy pre-waxed thread, or you can wax your own. The traditional wax is beeswax. It is a golden color and smells like honey. Modern waxes are white and a little harder than beeswax. Either kind works well.

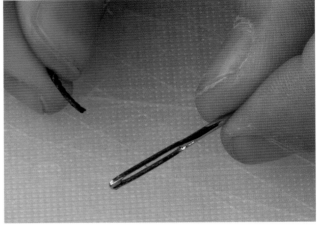

Hand-stitching needles for leather have a large eye and a blunt point.

Skills: Waxing Thread

Some sewing thread comes already waxed, other threads should be waxed before you sew with them.

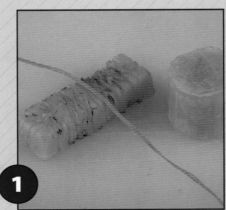

1

Wax the Thread
Use beeswax to prepare thread for sewing.

2

Cover the Thread
To wax your thread, pull a length of it across the beeswax block. Do it several times to cover the thread with wax.

Skills: Tying the Knot

Tie a square knot to end a seam or to join two pieces of waxed thread. The waxed thread likes to stick to itself, which helps you tie tight knots.

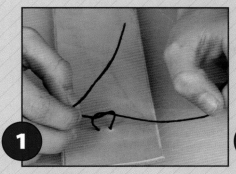

1

Overhand Knot
Make an overhand knot using waxed thread.

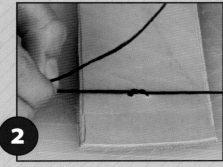

2

Pull Tight
Pull the knot tight.

3

Another Knot
Make a second knot on top of the first.

4

Pull Tight
Pull the knot tight.

Colored Thread

If you want to put a bit of color in your project you can use cotton embroidery thread. It comes in a rainbow of colors. Wax two strands of the thread together for strength. The soft beeswax helps the strands stick together.

Embroidery thread can be used to sew leather seams.

Supplies

Needles for Lacing

Flat lacing can be made of plastic or smooth leather. Both slide nicely through the punched holes. You can decide which to use by how you want your project to look. For thin flat lacing, we use the lok-eye needle. For heavier lacing, as used for the moccasin project (page 93), we use the screw-eye needle. This heavier lacing, called latigo lacing, is usually made of a brushed leather so it has a nap or fuzzy sueded look.

Screw eye needle for latigo lace ———

Lok-eye needle with flat lace ———

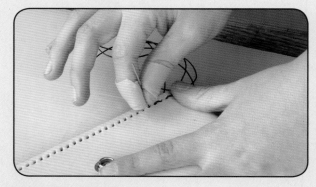

Helpful Hint:

Your fingers will become sore when sewing and lacing. You can protect them by putting band aids on your finger tips before you start to work.

Skills: Threading the Lok-Eye Needle

The lok-eye needle has a small prong that sticks into the lace to hold it; then you thread the lace through the eye. Loading a lok-eye needle is easiest to do with a buddy.

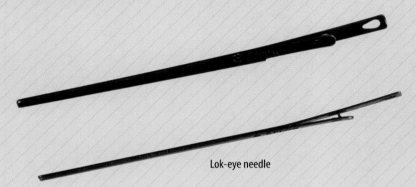

Lok-eye needle

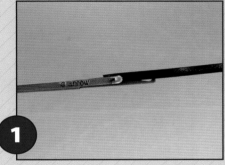

1

Open Slot
Gently bend the needle to open the prong slot and fit the end of the lace onto the prong.

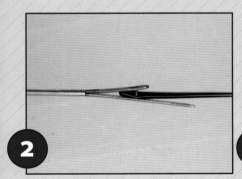

2

Lock the Lace
Let the needle close so the little prong can stab into the lace and lock it in.

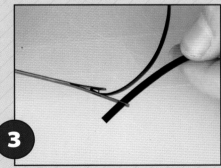

3

Free End
Thread the free end of the lace through the eye and pull it tight.

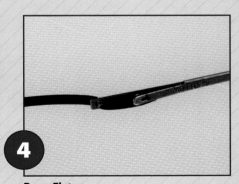

4

Press Flat
Press the lace flat against the needle and it should be held tight.

Skills: Threading the Screw Needle

The screw needle is very unusual because it has no eye for the lace. Instead it has a hole in the end with screw threads inside, so you can twist the needle onto the lacing.

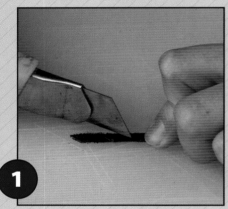

1

Cut a Point
Use the utility knife to cut a sharp point on the fat lacing.

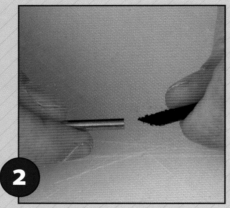

2

Feed the Needle
Feed the pointed lacing into the hole in the end of the needle.

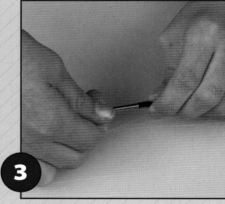

3

Twist Needle
Hold the lace tight and very close to its point, and twist the needle onto it. It is just like turning a nut onto a bolt.

Eyelets, (left), rivets (center), and snaps are packaged with the necessary setting tool and anvil you will need to install them in holes punched through the leather.

Metal Fasteners

Besides sewing and lacing, metal fasteners offer another way to join the parts of leather projects. We use three different kinds of metal fasteners:

- **Eyelets**, to make a strong hole
- **Rivets**, to permanently join two pieces of leather
- **Snaps**, which can be opened and closed

When we install a metal fastener, we say we have set it. Metal fasteners usually are sold along with the necessary setting tools (page 56). The metal fasteners fit into holes you punch in the leather. The skills of making holes and installing fasteners are covered on pages 57 through 59.

Supplies

Casing

Casing is wetting vegetable-tanned leather to soften it. Vegetable-tanned leather is the only leather you can stamp with tools to make pattern impressions, or groove with a swivel knife, after it has been cased.

For casing you need two things:

- a **sponge** of any kind,
- a **container** that is not metal.

Metal can cause stains on leather. Remember the plastic containers you collected from the kitchen? Use one of them.

Casing the leather means wetting it with a sponge so it can be tooled or folded.

Skills: Casing Leather

The trick with casing the leather is to get it a little damp, then wait while the leather absorbs the water and becomes almost dry again. Leather that is too dry is hard and you will not be able to make a clean fold nor make deep stamping impressions. On leather that is too wet, the impressions will swell back up and disappear. With practice you will get it just right.

1

Wet the Sponge
Wet your casing sponge, then squeeze out as much water as you can from it. You want the sponge to be just damp, not overly wet.

2

Wet the Leather
When you first touch the leather with the sponge you will see it darkens with the water. That is fine! Wet the whole piece of leather. If you wet only part and then stop, you will cause a stain.

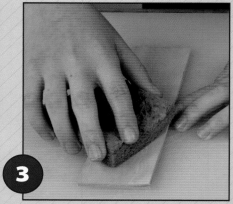

3

Wait
Now wait for the water to be absorbed into the leather. When the leather has returned to its natural color it is ready to work with.

Dry Enough Yet?

When cased leather looks dry, touch it to your face. If it feels cool there is still a little moisture in the leather so it is just right too use. If it feels warm, it is too dry to use.

Water Spots on Leather

If you drip water on vegetable-tanned leather you are not ready to use, it will stain as it dries. So as soon as you notice a stray drop, lightly moisten the whole piece of leather and rub a little extra water around the spot to blend it in. If you have done it soon enough, the water won't leave a mark. Every time you moisten vegetable-tanned leather it dries a little bit stiffer but the stiffness will go away when you oil your project (page 35).

Supplies

Coloring

You can color leather and you can draw colored designs on it, using dyes, markers, and acrylic paint. It is easiest to color and apply finishes on leather while the leather is still laying flat, before you cut it and shape it for your project.

Alcohol and water-based dyes are good for when you want to cover a larger surface. They come in a variety of colors and can be mixed together to create your own special colors. They are applied with a sponge. Remember to wear rubber gloves, or they will dye you, too!

For details, colored markers are easy to use and leave no mess to clean up. They come in many colors and sizes, from ultra fine to king size. Be sure to get markers that say permanent marker on the label. The colors won't fade from sunlight, or run if the leather gets wet. Try to find markers that are also labeled nontoxic because they have very little odor and are the best to use.

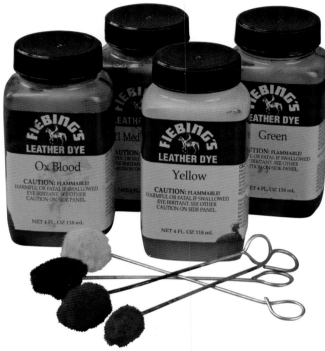

Dye the leather when you want to color large areas.

Acrylic paint creates a solid looking colored surface that hides the grain of the leather. We don't often use paint because it covers the natural beauty of the leather. But, in one step, paint gives a sealed finish to the leather that doesn't need any further work.

Permanent markers are good for detailing. Use acrylic paint when you want to hide the leather grain.

Skills: Dyeing Leather

The first coat dyes the top of the leather. Applying more coats makes the dye soak deeper into the leather. A second or even a third coat will produce a nice uniform color that is deep into the leather. Always start by dyeing a scrap of leather from your project to see how it will look. The same dye will look darker or lighter, or more red or orange, on different leathers. For some projects you might want to dye the back of the leather too.

More coats of dye make the colors darker and also smoother. These two sets of samples have one, two, and three coats.

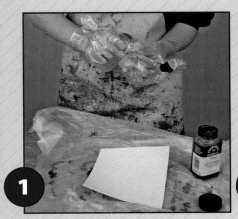

1

Preparing to Dye
Make sure to have all your supplies at hand: leather from your project, dye, and a small sponge or applicator. Put your gloves and apron on, and you are ready to start.

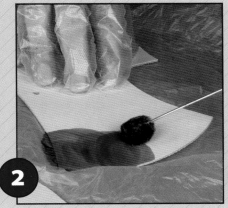

2

Rub Dye In
Dip your sponge or applicator into the dye. Now rub the dye into the leather using a circular motion, overlapping your strokes until you cover all the leather. Remember to do the edges! Let the dye soak into the leather for a minute or two.

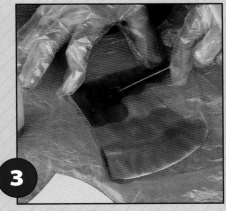

3

Evening the Color
Does the dye look blotchy? Leather naturally has softer spots that easily absorb the dye and harder spots that resist it. Apply a second coat, again using a circular motion, and try to blend in the blotches. You might want to do a third coat.

Supplies

Finishing

When you are shopping you will see that some leather comes already colored and sealed, and needs no additional care. But unfinished leathers, like the vegetable-tanned leather used for most of the projects in this book, need to have a finish put on.

For leather to remain soft and flexible, it needs to be conditioned by oiling. The products sold for oiling are combinations of oils and conditioners. Some leather workers use vegetable oil right from the grocery shelf. It does a wonderful job and is always available. Some leather items are complete with oiling. Some will need a finishing coat for added protection.

Suede should never be oiled because oil makes the fuzzy nap go flat. So that it resists water and stains, suede can be sprayed with a special sealer available at leather shops and shoe stores.

Vegetable oil is the simplest finishing treatment for leather. It darkens it and makes it gleam. Other leather finishes contain various mixtures of oil and wax.

Sun Block

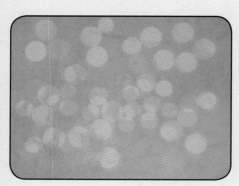

You can spread leather in the bright sunshine and it will suntan just like you do! The longer it is in the sun, the darker it will become, though after a few hours it will darken no more.

For a subtle effect, put objects on the leather while it tans in the sun. Covering part of the leather will leave that area light, just like your swim suit leaves tan lines on your body. This piece of leather had a handful of coins spread on it. Look at how the coins left their tan lines on the leather!

Oiling

For projects in this book, vegetable oil can be used to finish the leather. Wear rubber gloves when applying the oil, to protect your hands and so that when you remove your gloves you don't have any oil on your hands. Oily fingers will leave fingerprints on unfinished leather.

Put the oil in a small bowl. Use a soft cloth or sponge, dip it into the oil, and squeeze out the extra oil. Then apply the oil using a circular motion and overlapping your strokes until you get a uniform look.

Let the oil be absorbed into leather before using. If a top finish is needed, it is best to wait a day or two before applying it, to be sure all of the oil has soaked in.

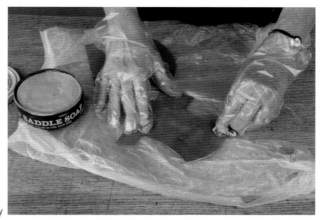

Apply water-resistant finishes following the directions on the can. This waxy material is being rubbed into the leather.

Waterproofing

You can apply top finishes over your oiled leather to provide you with a water resistant or waterproof finish, and to make your leather look mellow or shiny. You will need to read the labels on the bottles of finish to see what kind it is, how to apply it, and how it looks when dried.

There is a difference between water resistant and waterproof leather. If you drip liquid onto water resistant finish, it will stay on top of the leather for a while but will eventually seep in and it can cause a watermark. A waterproof finish seals so tight that liquids just roll off. The waterproof finish is great for leatherwork that will be used outside because rain or snow will not harm it. Waterproof finish does need to be reapplied from time to time, depending on how much it has been exposed to moisture, to keep it waterproof.

Here is a fun test for your finishes. Oil and finish a piece of scrap leather just as you think you would like to do on your project. Then drip some water on it. Keep track of how long it takes to seep through to the leather and darken it under the finish. If it doesn't seep through at all, you know that you have made a good waterproof finish.

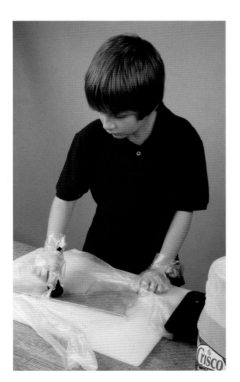

CHAPTER 3

Leatherworking Tools

Leather working uses many different tools. A few, such as pliers and scissors, you may already have in your home or workshop. You can get the rest at your local hobby center, fabric store, or leather supplier. Sometimes you can find the special tools at yard sales and in antique shops. Ask your friends and their parents, too–they might have tools you can borrow.

As you learn about the tools, handle them often, and get to know them. Let them become your good friends.

These leatherworking tools are all you need to make the eleven projects in this book, and many more besides. The white work surface is an ordinary kitchen cutting board, made of plastic.

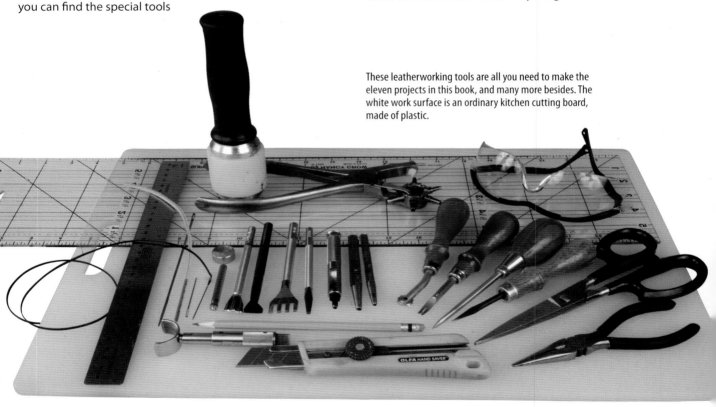

Getting Your Tools Ready

Having clean tools for leather working is very important. Leather can be stained by oil, metal, dirt, and water. Use a soft clean rag to wipe each tool off. Be sure to clean all of the little nooks and crannies.

Think of your work table as a tool also. Keep it clean and free of dirt, oils, and water drips. Avoid having food or beverage on your work table while you work. An accidental spill can spot your leather or damage your tools.

Tools for Safety: Think About It

Leatherworking is a safe and most enjoyable hobby when you follow a few rules and use tools safely. First check that you have your safety tools ready. Then, form the habit of pausing to think before you do anything with tools. Review in your mind what you are going to do before taking action.

Your mind is your first and most important safety tool. Start your thoughts big and think until you reach the smallest details. First look around you–do you have enough space to comfortably work? How about the lighting–can you see clearly? Think of your body and how you are dressed–do you have dangling hair or sleeves? You don't want to catch them on a tool, sew them into your project, or dip them in your dye! Are your toes safely covered with shoes? You wouldn't want to drop a heavy mallet or a sharp knife on your bare toe. Where are your hands placed? Make sure no fingers are ever in the path of your cutting knife or your sewing needle. Watch out for that little pinkie finger!

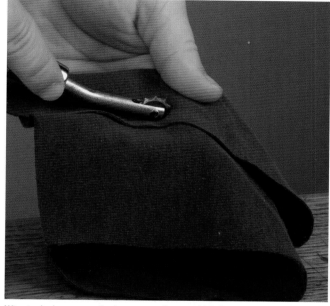

Wipe tools clean on a soft, clean rag, such as an old T-shirt.

Safety

Hair

If you have long hair tuck it under a cap or tie it back when you are working. You don't want it to get into your eyes, tools, or stitching.

Eyes

Wear eye protection anytime you are working with hammers or mallets and other striking tools, or helping a buddy work. Something you tap might go flying.

Nose and Lungs

The supplies recommended for use in this book are nontoxic and not too smelly. You might wish to wear a disposable dust mask when cutting the leather, especially suede, because of the little fibers that get in the air.

Hands

Wear disposable plastic or rubber gloves when using dyes and finishes. When cutting, always take note of where all of your fingers are. Pause before using any cutting tool to look at how and where your hands are positioned. Some leather workers wear gloves made from metal mesh to protect their hands from cuts. You can get these gloves at some stores that sell woodworking supplies.

Feet

Wear shoes when doing leather work. Some tools are pointy and sharp, others are heavy. Bare feet or feet in socks need to be protected. Sandals will not give enough protection but sneakers are fine.

The leather-cutting surface on this old work table is a plastic kitchen cutting board. The plywood surface is for tooling leather.

Worktable

The worktable does not need to be a special table but it needs to be sturdy. On it you need to place two different surfaces: one for cutting leather and punching holes, the other for tooling leather.

The surface for cutting leather and punching holes could be a poly kitchen cutting board, or a linoleum floor square. The surface is to protect your tool's cutting edges, and also to protect your worktable top.

The other surface needs to be very hard, for using when you are tooling the leather. The harder the surface the better you can make your tooling impressions. A piece of Masonite board works well. The ultimate surface is a polished stone, a foot square and $1\frac{1}{2}$" thick.

Tools

Measuring and Layout

Learning to measure and lay out patterns is fun. It is a skill that will help you in so many ways. You can make patterns for woodworking, posters, and games. You can measure how tall your buddies are! You will need several different tools for measuring and marking:

- **Pencil** for marking on paper and leather,

- **Paper or cardboard** for your patterns,

- **A clear, gridded ruler** for drawing, and

- **A metal ruler** for cutting against.

You will need to make patterns for your leather parts. Draw your patterns with pencil. Don't use a pen because it can leave marks that will transfer onto your leather as permanent stains. Use your clear ruler for drawing your pattern. You can find a clear ruler at fabric and craft stores. It is marked in inches and with a grid to help you measure and keep your lines straight and square. Use your metal ruler for cutting. It is strong and will not be nicked by your cutter.

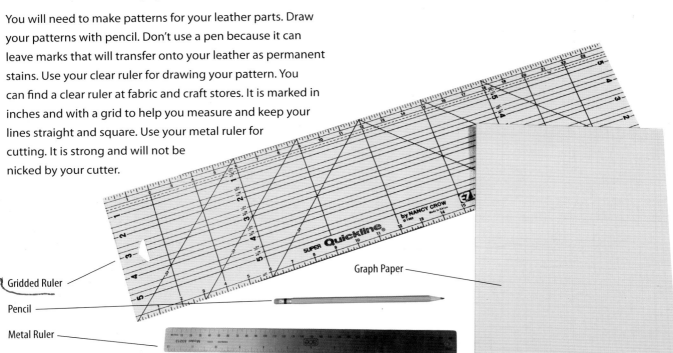

Gridded Ruler

Graph Paper

Pencil

Metal Ruler

These tools help you make full-size patterns on paper, which you can transfer onto the leather.

Skills: Making a Pattern

As you make your projects, you will find there are many details to put on the patterns, such as the position of snaps, fold lines, and holes. For a pattern you might want to use over and over, make it on heavy paper or cardboard that will last. Cardboard from a cereal box or from a manila file folder is great.

Our practice pattern is for a book marker. It is a simple pattern that can be helpful for working out your stamping ideas and color ideas. Book markers are nice to make because they are small and allow you to experiment with different tools and techniques. You can give them as gifts or keep them as your own personal reference library. Some leather workers have drawers of book markers and other little leather samples for future reference.

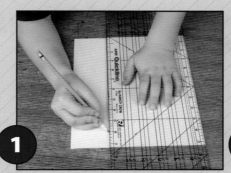

1

Draw a Straight Line
On your paper use the clear, gridded ruler to draw a line seven inches long. Hold your pencil tight against the ruler to get a straight line.

2

Draw a Square Line
Turn the ruler like this to make your next two lines. Look through the ruler and line up its grid on the first line so that this line will be perpendicular to your first. Make the lines two inches long.

3

Parallel Lines
Draw the last line between the ends of the two short lines. See how the ruler's grid helped to keep your lines square and parallel?

4

Label the Pattern
You have just drawn your first official pattern! Cut it out and label it BOOK MARKER so you can keep it and use it again and again. Make a few extra patterns now—you will be using them later.

Cutting Tools

There are three different kinds of tools you can use for cutting leather:

■ utility knife with disposable blades,

■ rotary cutter from the fabric store, and

■ leather cutting shears.

The most versatile cutting tool is the utility knife, which you can get at your local hardware store. The utility knife will cut any weight leather. When the blade becomes dull you can exchange it for a sharp blade or snap off its tip for a new sharp edge.

Leather shears are a heavy duty pair of scissors. They cut lightweight and mediumweight leather nicely, but you need strong hands to use them. The rotary cutter is found at craft and fabric stores and is good for cutting lightweight and soft leathers.

Utility Knife

Leather Shears

Rotary Cutter

A utility knife with a breakaway blade is excellent for cutting straight lines in leather. When it gets dull, just snap off the blade tip and you'll have a new sharp edge.

With scissors, you can cut leather into any shape you like. Some people prefer the rotary cutter for straight lines in thin materials.

Helpful Hint:

To cut small pieces of leather, stick them down to your cutting board with two-sided tape. Plastic carpet tape works very well. Peel the tape off the leather when you are done cutting.

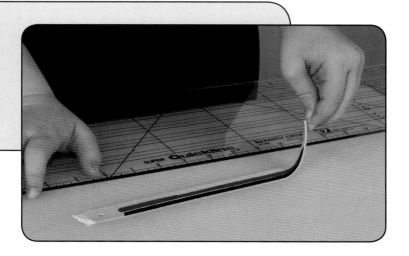

Skills: Cutting with the Utility Knife

Practice cutting a scrap piece of leather.

Place your ruler-holding hand in the correct position and think about what you are going to do: put your cutter edge next to the ruler and pull the cutter along the ruler. Always keep a little pressure against the ruler with the cutter to get a straight cut. However, too much pressure and the ruler could slide.

To cut the leather, pull the utility knife along the straight edge.

Cutting Safety

Leather cutting tools need to be very sharp to cut smooth clean lines. A sharp tool is easier to pull through the leather, so it is safer than a dull tool. Cut against the clear, gridded ruler or better yet, the metal ruler. Choose the ruler that will best help you hold your project down without any slipping. Place your ruler along the line over your pattern so if you slip, you'll cut into your scrape and not into the project.

Place your holding hand on the opposite side of the ruler from where you are cutting. Holding the ruler on the same side as you are cutting can cause an accident! Hold the ruler down very firmly. To cut along the ruler, start where you are holding and stop at the end of where you are holding. Move your holding hand so it will again be alongside where you want to cut, and then continue cutting. This is the steadiest way to hold your ruler so it doesn't slip. The ruler can slip when you hold too far away from where you are cutting.

Hold the ruler firmly down on the leather so it can't move when you cut against it. Keep your holding hand away from the cutting line.

Be careful how you hold the ruler! Don't place your fingers in the knife's path.

Mallet

The mallet is used for many different purposes in leather working, including tapping the hole punch, setting snaps and rivets, and tapping stamping tools. The mallet shown is made of aluminum with a hard nylon head. You also can use a wooden mallet, but in leather working we do not use a metal hammer. A hard metal hammer can damage tools, and because of the moisture in the leather it could start to rust, which would stain the leather.

Hold your mallet with a firm but not overly tight grip. Keep relaxed. For light taps, swing from your wrist. For heavy taps, swing from your elbow. Using your workbench top as a striking surface, practice swinging from your wrist and elbow until you get used to the feel of the mallet.

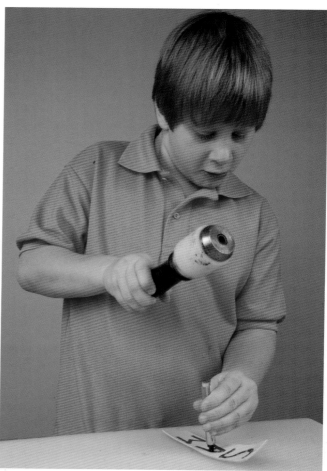

Keep your eye on the target when you strike with the mallet.

Nylon round head mallet

Hole Punch

In leather working you will make many holes. Snaps and rivets need holes to be set into, heavy lacing needs holes, and you can make interesting decorative patterns on your projects by punching holes.

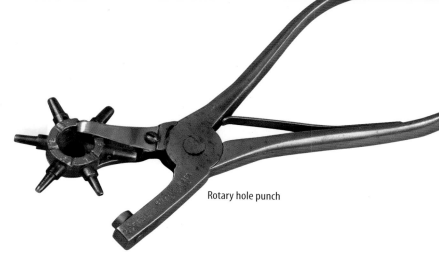

Rotary hole punch

There are two different basic tools for punching holes:

- the **single-hole punch**, and

- the **rotary punch**.

The single-hole punch comes in different sizes and you strike it with a mallet. The single-hole punch is versatile because it can be used on any weight leather and anywhere on the leather. Some single hole punches have interchangeable tips so the same tool can be used to make a variety of different-sized holes. The rotary punch is like pliers with different-sized punches on a rotating wheel. You turn the wheel to the size hole you want to punch. Then by squeezing the handles like a pair of pliers, you punch the hole. The rotary punch works best on thin leather, for holes near the edges.

Squeeze rotary punches like they were pliers. Turn the head to select different sizes. They work best on thin leather.

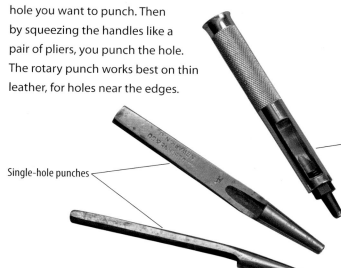

Single-hole punches

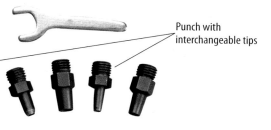

Punch with interchangeable tips

Some single-hole punches make one size of hole (left). Some have interchangeable tips for making holes of many different sizes. Single-hole punches work in leather of any thickness.

Skills: How to Punch a Hole

The single-hole punch is the first tool we will use with the mallet. The leather should be dry when punching holes. The holes will be easier to punch because dry leather is slick, and wet leather is sticky. Place the leather on your cutting board to make holes. This will help keep your hole punching tool sharp by giving it a soft surface to strike.

Choose the Punch
When you are punching a hole for a metal fastener, you can check the size by holding the fastener up to the punch.

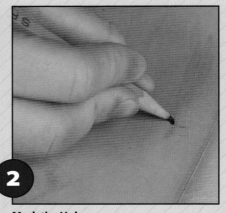

Mark the Hole
Use a pencil to mark where you want the hole. Make a dot with the point of the pencil to show the center of the hole.

Position your Punch
Place the punch so it covers the pencil mark. Hold the punch straight up and down, then tap it lightly with the mallet– just enough to make a dent.

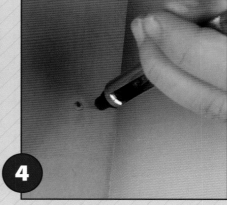

It Looks Like This
Move the punch away and look to see where you made the dent. It should look like a bull's eye–a circle punch dent with the pencil dot in the middle. If it doesn't, move the punch, tap again, and look again.

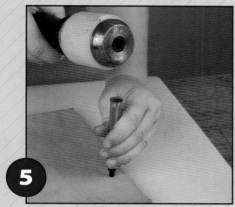

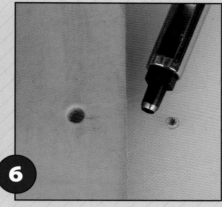

5

Punch the Hole

Place your hole punch back into the circle dent. Then hold the punch straight and pound it with the mallet. It might take a few hard taps to punch through the leather.

6

Leather Dot

When you lift the punch off the leather, a little circle of leather will be inside the tool. That's fine, it will come out through the side-slot when you punch more holes.

Hole Punch Practice

For fun, print your initials on a leather piece with a pencil—make the letters an inch tall. Then make pencil dots spaced on your pencil lines. Punch the holes. Can you read your initials?

You can also practice punching holes with two pieces of leather glued together back to back. This is how you will cut holes for some of the sewing projects. Punching through two thicknesses of leather uses more muscle than punching just one.

Stitching Awl and Fid

A fid is for marking measurements and hole locations, and enlarging holes for easier stitching and lacing. It has a blunt point. A stitching awl is like a fid, except it has a four-sided diamond-shaped cross-section, with sharp edges and a very sharp point. Be careful not to jab your finger while handling it. The stitching awl is for cutting small holes. The beveled sides of the stitching awl can be sharpened.

Awls and fids have beveled sides with sharp corners, so they can cut and enlarge holes in leather.

Hold the stitching awl or the fid with the handle resting against the heel of the hand, your thumb and index finger holding the neck. Your other fingers grip the handle.

To use the stitching awl to make a hole, place your leather on your cutting surface. Mark the hole position with just a pin-prick of the awl. Hold the awl firmly, straight up and down in all directions, and push down. Push until you have gone through the leather and the point sticks, but just a bit, into your cutting surface. Now give the awl a small, quarter-turn twist to release it and pull it back out.

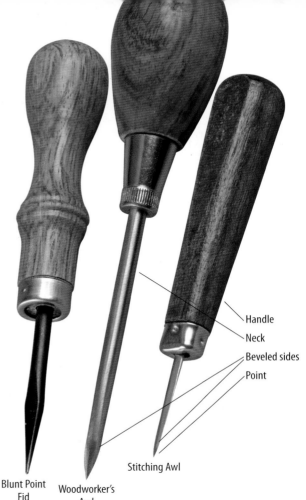

Handle
Neck
Beveled sides
Point

Stitching Awl

Blunt Point
Fid

Woodworker's
Awl

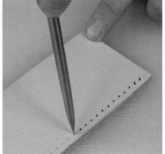

Use the awl to make sewing holes in leather.

Helpful Hint:

When not using the stitching awl you can protect its point and your fingers by stabbing it into an eraser.

Lacing Chisel

Lacing chisels cut little slits in the leather for you to use for lacing. They are made as single-prong chisels for corner slits, and multi-prong chisels for straight lines. For the projects in this book, get a single-prong chisel and a four-prong chisel that each make 1/8" wide slits.

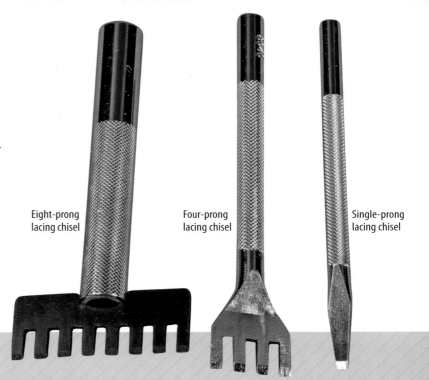

Eight-prong lacing chisel

Four-prong lacing chisel

Single-prong lacing chisel

Skills: Using the Lacing Chisel

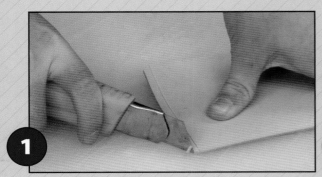

1

Start in the Corner
Let's start making the slits from the corner of your leather. Trim the point off the corner.

2

Mark Lacing Line
Mark a line with the fid 1/8" from the edge. This is the lacing line.

3

Place the Chisel
Use the single-prong chisel. Place it as shown in photo. Hold the chisel straight up and down.

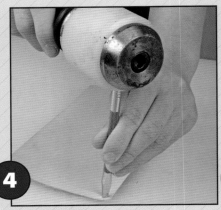

4

Strike the Chisel
Strike it with the mallet until you have pierced through. It might take a few taps. Don't use a metal hammer to strike the chisel, it can damage the tool.

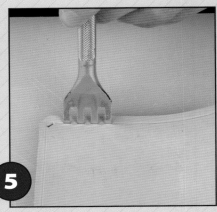

5

Start the Line
To start the long line, space the four-prong chisel one prong width away from the corner slit. Set the chisel on the marked line and tap it with the mallet. Do you feel how much more strength you need to punch four holes compared to one hole?

6

Continue the Line
To continue your straight line position the chisel's end prong in the last slit. Now tap again with the mallet and you will have made an additional three holes. Continue until you are close to the next corner.

7

Space into Corners
When you are close to the corner, change to the single prong chisel. Then work backward to your last slit—eyeballing to space the slits out as evenly as possible. It is easy to get confused between what is a slit and what is not, and a little unevenness is expected.

Skills: Lacing the Leather

You now have a punched leather part ready for lacing. Cut your lace four times longer than the length you are going to lace. Load the lok-eye needle with flat lacing, as on page 27. Watch that your lace doesn't twist. Keep it smooth as you go around the edges and corners.

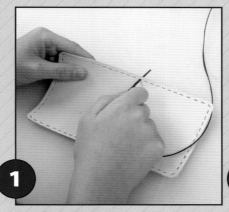

1

Start from the Front
Start lacing from the front side of your leather. Pull the lace through until there is a 4" tail remaining.

2

Over the Edge
Go through the next hole from the same side of the leather, so the lace wraps over the edge. Keep the lace flat and smooth.

3

Capture the End
Leave the first three stitches loose. Place your 4" end under the loose stitches. Pull it to the back. Now pull the stitches tight to capture the short end of the lace.

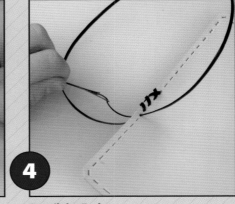

4

Detail the End
For a nice look, try to make an "x" shape with the loops of lacing where they started. Trim off the the rest of the loose end.

5

Sew the Seam
Now continue sewing your seam, pulling each stitch tight as you go.

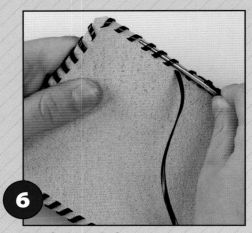

6

Trap the Loose End
Finish the end of the seam the same as the beginning but in reverse order. Leave the last three stitches loose, and run your threaded needle underneath them. Pull each loop, one by one, tight on top of your loose end.

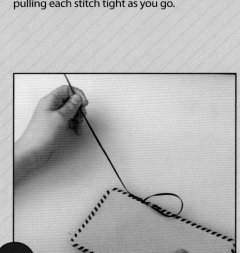

7

Tighten
Pull the threaded lace tight underneath the loops.

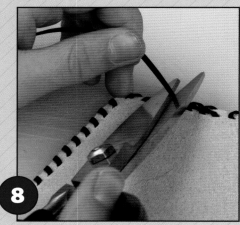

8

Trim
Snip off the extra length close to the seam.

Stitch Marker

A stitch marker is a rotary wheel tool for marking the equal spacing of stitches. Stitch markers come with different numbers of prongs on them. The number stamped on the tool tells you how many stitches the prongs will mark per inch. For the projects in this book, the #5 tool is the best, because we will be using heavy thread. Numbers 6 and 7 are for thinner threads.

Skills: Stitch Marking

To make a line for stitching, lightly mark the line with your fid. Just dent the top surface; don't scratch it deep.

1

Mark the Line
Mark the line at least as far from the edge as your leather is thick. It will be closer to the edge on lightweight leather, and farther in on heavyweight leather.

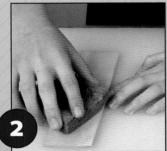

2

Case the Leather
Lightly case the leather where you have marked your line before running the stitch marker on the leather. This will help the marker make a deep impression.

3

Run the Marker
Mark only on the top side of the leather. Carefully follow the line, or use the metal ruler as shown here. If you get off the line, go back and start again. Stray stitching marks usually disappear next to the heavy thread.

4

Punch the Marks
Use your stitching awl (page 48) to punch holes in every mark you made. See how the awl's cuts are made at an angle. This prevents cutting one mark into another. More leather around each hole makes for a stronger seam.

Skills: Sewing a Running Stitch

A running stitch with waxed thread is a very neat way of making a seam in leather. Use the stitch marker and stitching awl to lay out the sewing and cut holes for the needle (previous page). You can use one color of thread, or more than one, so it's also a way of decorating your project. To learn how to thread your sewing needle, see page 28.

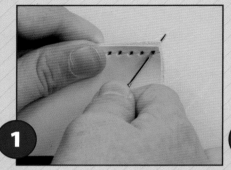

1

Start on Top

Use your handsewing needle with waxed thread. Start from the top side of the leather, at one end of the punched line of holes or slits. Push down through the first slit, leaving a 6" tail of thread.

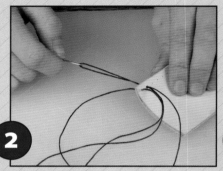

2

Up from Below

Now push the needle through the next hole. Continue stitching this way, down from the top and up from the bottom. Stitch until you reach the last hole of your seam.

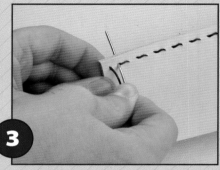

3

Back Stitch the End

To end your seam and secure your thread, do back stitching, sewing back over your last few stitches. See how the thread tightly fills the holes? Back stitch for three or four holes, ending with your thread on the back of the leather. Carefully trim off the long thread close to the leather.

4

Back Stitch the Start

Now go back to the start of the seam and thread the needle with that 6" tail. Backstitch here too.

5

Make It Stronger

Trim off the extra thread. You have done your first seam with the running stitch. To make a stronger seam you can make a second running stitch using the same holes and filling in the spaces between your first stitches.

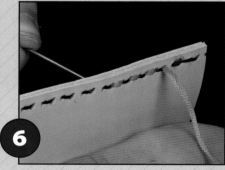

6

Add a Color

For a decorative stitching your can do your first running stitch with one color thread and then your second running stitch with a contrasting color.

Edge Beveler

We use the edger beveler to cut a thin sliver off the edge of leather. This is so the edge can be finished and will wear better. Edge bevelers come in different sizes so you can trim a small edge off thin leather and a larger edge off thicker leather. For the leather in these projects, use a #2 beveler.

Hold the leather firmly to your worktable. Start beveling at the bottom of one side, pushing the tool away from you. To make a neat corner, start the next side from the stopping corner of the one before. Turn the leather so your next cut will start where you just ended. Neat, right? You have three more corners to perfect your style!

Skills: Beveling Edges

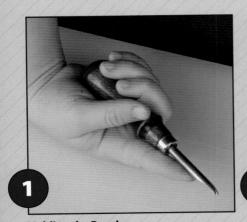

1

Holding the Beveler
Hold the handle of the edge beveler comfortably in your palm. To push the tool down into the leather, place your index finger on the neck in back of the cutting edge.

2

Holding the Leather
Hold the tool at the angle shown. Keep your hand holding the leather away from the edge you're cutting. Hold the leather down firmly!

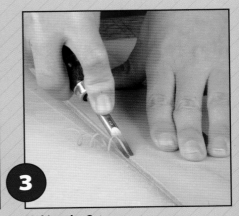

3

Making the Cut
The beveler will only cut on a forward push. Practice holding the tool at an angle while also pushing push down with your index finger and forward with your hand, all at the same time. Thin leather is a challenge to bevel; heavy leather is easier.

Rivet and Snap Setters

We use setters and anvils to fasten or "set" rivets and snaps onto the leather. Rivets make a permanent connection, while snaps can be opened and closed. To set a rivet or snap, you must first punch a hole for the stud to pass through. You position the rivet or snap parts with the hole in the leather, place it on the little anvil, then strike the setter with your mallet. The setters mushroom the metal parts, so they clamp onto the leather.

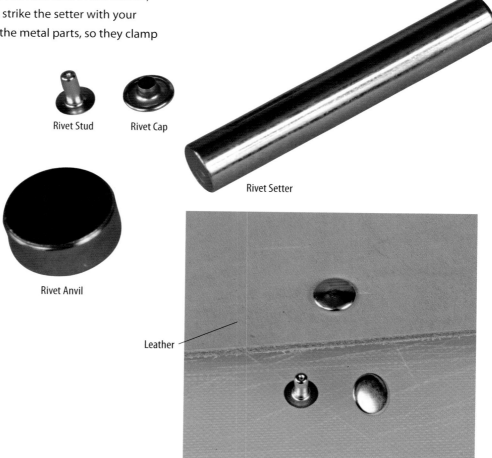

Rivet Stud

Rivet Cap

Rivet Setter

Rivet Anvil

Leather

Skills: Setting Rivets

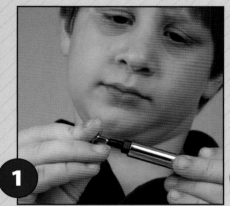

1

Select the Hole Punch
The hole should fit snugly. Hold the rivet post up to the hole punch to be sure it is the right size.

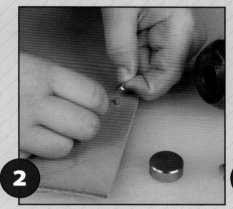

2

Position the Rivet Parts
Place your parts in order: stud with post side up, leather over the stud post, then the rivet cap on the stud post.

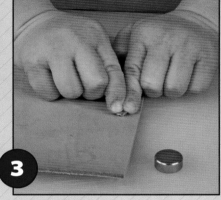

3

Press Tight
Push it snug with your thumb, to help it go together straight.

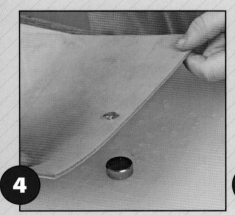

4

Position the Anvil
Place the anvil flat side up with the rivet stud on it.

5

Position the Anvil
Place the setter over the cap with its concave or hollow side down. The hollow in the setter fits the curve in the cap.

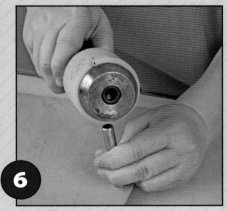

6

Strike the Setter
Now hold the mallet straight up and down and strike the setter sharply. Check the fit of the rivet. Is it snug? If not, line it up again and strike until it is.

Skills: Setting Snaps

Setting a snap is like setting a rivet but you do it on two parts you want to open and close again. A size 24 (or line 24) snap is a good size to use. It doesn't matter what side you do first. Remember that at first the snap will be hard to open and close, but it will loosen up as it wears.

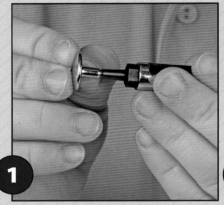

1

Punch the Hole
Start with the stud side. Punch a hole for the eyelet post to pass through. Not too small, not too big, but just right: hold the post up to the setter to check the size.

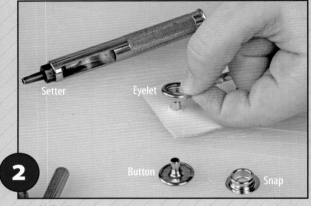

2

Stack the Parts
Place the anvil with the concave side up. Place your eyelet post on the anvil, post side up. Fit the punched hole in your leather over the eyelet post. Add the eyelet with the flat side down. It will slip right on the eyelet post and slide down onto the leather.

Anvil

Eyelet Post

Button

Eyelet

Snap

Setter

3

Swat the Setter

Place the setter over the eyelet post with its pointed side down. The point on the setter flares the post out so it clamps the two parts onto the leather. Strike the setter sharply with the mallet. Check the fit. Is it snug? If not, line it up again and hit until it is.

4

Orient the Button Side

Now let's do the button side. Punch a hole. Stack the parts. Before you set the snap, make sure the parts are placed in the right order. It's easy to get it backward, but not so easy to remove the snap to do over.

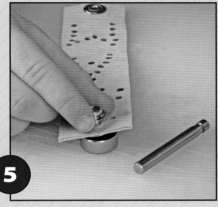

5

Set the Button Side

Place the anvil with its concave or dished side up. Fit the button into the anvil's dish, post up, then the leather, and finally socket with the open side up. Place the setter with its pointed side down and strike with the mallet until it's snug.

Tools

Stamping Tools

We use stamping and carving tools to make decorative designs on the leather. The leather must be vegetable tanned tooling leather. The traditional patterns are of flowers and leaves, with a decorative border. Try to see some tooled saddles at your local farm implement store or tack shop so you can also feel the texture made by this tooling. Tooling helps protect the saddle because it compacts the leather, making it stronger.

There are hundreds of patterns of stamping tools that are ready made, each with a special purpose. Finding things you can use as your own stamping tools is great fun—it is like going on a treasure hunt. Look for hard objects that can be tapped with a mallet without breaking, such as bolt heads, nuts, large paperclips, and many other things you can find around the house. You can make a holder for small things so you don't tap your fingers (see page 61).

Ready-made stamping tools can be stored and organized in a wooden block with drilled holes. There are hundreds of patterns.

This piece of tooled leather is a work in progress. On the right, the flowers and leaves have been outlined with the swivel knife. On the left, they have been shaded and given depth by stamping.

Protect your eyes by wearing goggles or a face shield when stamping.

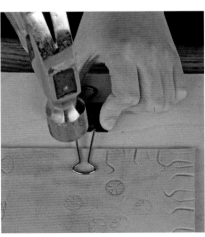

These patterns were made using a large binder clip and the head of a bolt.

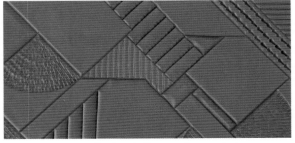

This geometric pattern has been knife-cut and stamped using traditional stamping tools.

Skills: Stamping a Pattern

First put on your safety goggles! Case a piece of leather. Set out your stamping tools, and use your plastic-faced or wooden mallet.

Practice holding the stamping tool straight up and down. Experiment with how hard you strike the tool to make a deeper impression.

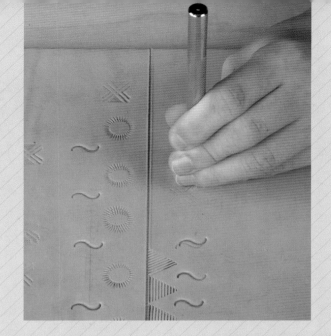

1

Stamping with Ready-Made Tools
Practice stamping on a scrap of cased leather. Try striking the tool harder and softer, and look at the impressions you get.

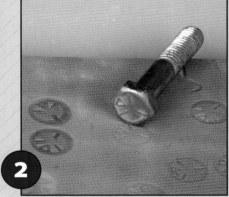

2

Stamp with a Bolt
Try using a bolt to tap a pattern. A bolt is long enough to hold easily and safely when striking with the mallet.

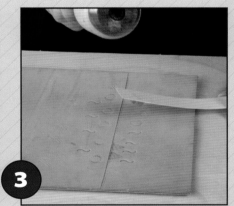

3

Stamp with Small Objects
To make an impression with a small object such as a nut or washer, use doublestick tape to mount the object on a strip of cardboard. The cardboard makes a handle so you don't hit your fingers.

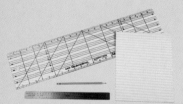

CHAPTER 4
Projects

Bookmark

A bookmark is a quick and useful project that is also fun to make. It can be a great gift for your friends, family, teachers, everyone. You can make the bookmarks as plain or colorful as you want. Bookmarks also can be a great way to keep samples of different kinds of leather and leatherworking techniques.

To make the project you will need to practice measuring skills, (page 40), cutting leather (page 43), beveling edges (page 55), and coloring with markers (page 32). You could follow the same steps to make computer mouse pads, a writing pad for your desk, or a gift of dinner place mats.

Tools

Layout Tools

Beveling Tool

Utility Knife

Cutting Surface

Leather Pattern: Bookmark

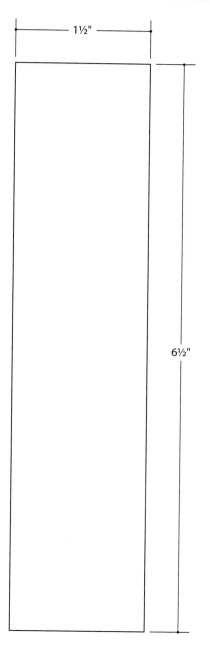

1½"

6½"

Leather
- 4/5 oz. vegetable-tanned cowhide scrap, rough size 4" x 7" for two bookmarks

Supplies
- Permanent colored markers
- #24 Snaps (If you plan to make a wristband)

Skills
- Measuring
- Cutting
- Beveling
- Coloring

Making: A Bookmark

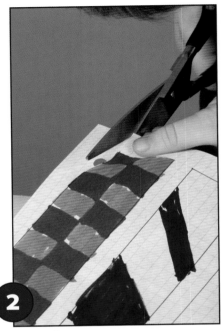

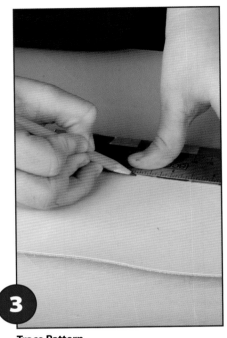

1

Draw and Color Pattern

You drew a bookmark pattern when learning how to measure (page 41). You can use that pattern, or you can make another. Use markers to draw and color a design on your pattern.

2

Cut Out Pattern

Use scissors, or a utility knife and straight edge, to cut out your pattern. Try to cut right on your layout lines.

3

Trace Pattern

Place the pattern where you want it on the leather—maybe there are defects you want to avoid or beauty marks you want to include. Then trace the pattern onto the leather. Use the ruler to make your lines straight and clear.

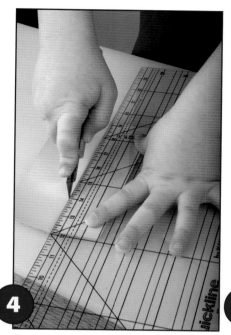

4

Cut Leather

Place the leather on your cutting surface, and line up your ruler on your cutting line. Review cutting safety on page 43. Hold the ruler firmly. Now cut down the line with your utility knife. If the first cut doesn't go all the way through, carefully line up your tools again and make a second pass. Cut all four sides.

5

Bevel Edges

Use the beveling tool to cut the sharp edges off the leather, as explained on page 55. Hold the leather firmly on the worktable and start beveling at one corner, pushing the tool away from you. Bevel all four sides.

6

Color the Bookmark

Now is the time for your imagination! Use your extra paper patterns to experiment with the markers to make different patterns with different colors. You can make geometric designs, or personalize with friends' and family names. Try drawing your pet!

Project

Mystery Wrist Band

This wrist band truly is a mystery, a braid made in the middle of one piece of leather. This project is a challenge that will amaze your friends. To have it come out right, you will need to follow the braiding instructions exactly.

Do the braiding a few times— braid and unbraid your band for practice. The leather will become softer and easier to braid each time. Before long you will be able to do it with your eyes closed.

To make the project you will need to practice measuring, (page 40), cutting leather (page 43), and punching holes and setting a snap (page 58). Once you learn the technique, you could make a collar for your pet, a belt by making the braided band longer and wider, or longer yet for a very special pet leash.

Tools

Mallet

Utility Knife

Layout Tools

Cutting Surface

Hole Punch

Snap Setter

Leather Pattern: Mystery Wrist Band

Leather
- For a tough wrist band use 4/5 oz. vegetable-tanned leather; for a smooth fit use 4/5 oz. cowhide suede split; rough size 1" x 12"

Supplies
- #24 snap
- Red and black markers
- Two-sided tape

Skills
- Measuring
- Cutting
- Coloring
- Punching holes
- Setting snap
- Braiding leather

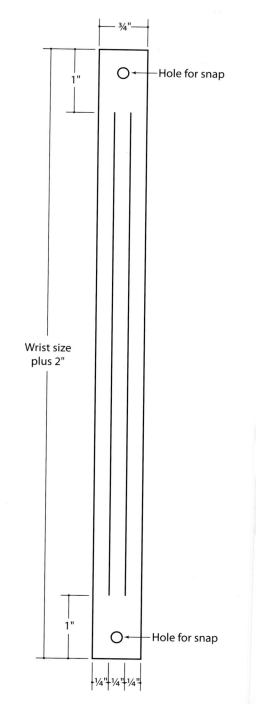

¾"

1"

Hole for snap

Wrist size plus 2"

1"

Hole for snap

¼" ¼" ¼"

Making: Mystery Wrist Band

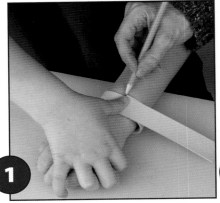

Measure Your Wrist
Start with a strip of leather 1" wide and 12" long, and wrap it around your wrist. Ask your buddy to mark the length around your wrist.

Cut the Leather to Length
The band needs extra length for the snaps and the braiding, so add 2" to the length you marked, and cut the strip to this size.

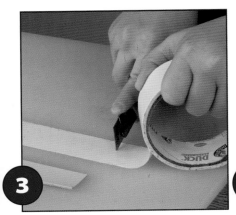

Tape It Down
You're about to cut slits in the leather, so use two-sided carpet tape to stick the leather onto your work surface.

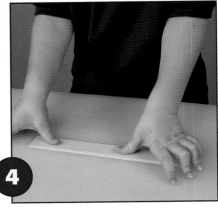

Stick It Tight
Press it down tight. You don't want it to move around while you cut it.

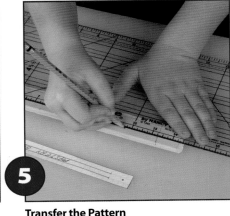

Transfer the Pattern
Copy the pattern from this book onto a piece of paper, adjusting it to the length of your leather band. Then use the gridded ruler to draw the pattern onto the leather.

Cut the Slits

Use the clear, gridded ruler to help you cut the two inside slits in the leather band, then cut the outside of the band. Leave it taped down.

Punch Holes

Mark the holes for the snap. Punch the two holes, as explained on page 58. Leave the band taped down!

Color the Leather

To help learn how to braid, color the strands. Use permanent markers to color the middle strand red and the right strand black. Leave the left strand natural color. Now you can remove the band from the cutting surface and peel the tape off it.

Set Snaps

Set the snaps following the instructions on page 58. Be sure to put the top button of the snap onto the top side of the band. Layer your snap parts down from there to keep them in the right order.

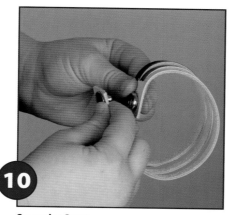

Snap the Snap

Test the snap to be sure it works the way you want.

Making: Mystery Wrist Band

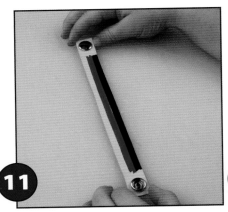

11

Braiding
Are you ready to do the twist? Hold the band so your strands are natural color on the left, red in the middle, and black on the right. Be ready to laugh as your fingers feel clumsy learning this challenge. You might feel as if you are all thumbs!

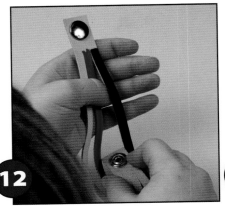

12

Turn End Up
Turn the bottom of the band up toward you and feed it between the red and black strands.

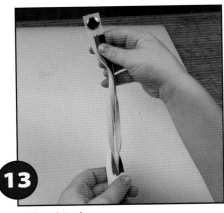

13

Pull and Push
Pull the band taut between your two hands. Push the twist you just made down to the bottom so the top of the strands are straight and flat.

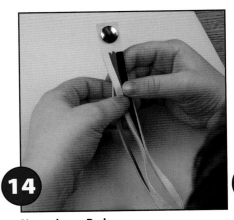

14

Natural over Red
Working at the top of the band, move the natural strip over the red.

15

Black over Natural
Lift the black strand over the natural strand.

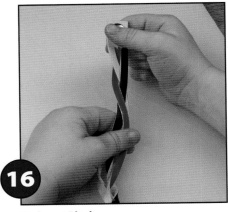

16

Red over Black
Bring the red strand over the black. Keep the strands face up and smooth while you are twisting them. This is challenging!

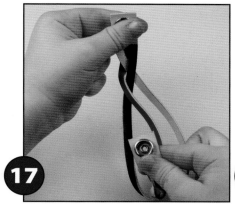

17

Turn Again
Now lift the bottom end of the band up toward you and feed it back through between the red and black strands, just below where you have been twisting.

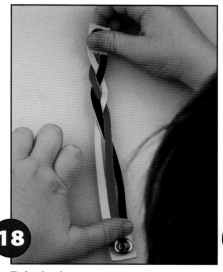

18

Twist Again
Move the twists up to the top. You'll see you have made one complete braid. Smooth the lower strands out flat and in their beginning order, natural, red, black.

19

Another Turn
Lift the bottom of the band and feed the end through the space between the black and red strands, just as you did before in Step 10.

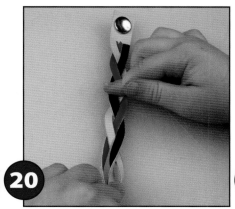

20

Another Braid
Bring the natural strand over the red, the black over the natural, and the red over the black, also as you did before in Steps 11 through 14.

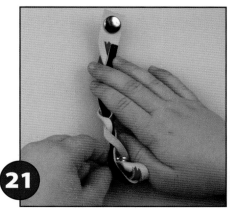

21

The Last Turn
For the last time, lift the bottom of the band and feed the end through the space between the black and red strands.

22

Finishing Touch
When you have finished the steps for the second time, smooth the braids out and make them evenly spaced. Try the mystery band on your wrist. Isn't it amazing?

Project

Belt with Buckle

It is very handy to know how to make a belt. Belts can be made in so many different ways, narrow or wide, for work or school, in any color. A belt can be sized small as a collar for your pet, or very small for a wrist band. Belts are wonderful gifts that you can personalize for that special person. The buckle is held onto the belt by snaps so you can change your belt buckles.

To make this project you will need to practice measuring and layout skills (page 40), cutting leather with a knife (page 43), beveling edges (page 55), punching holes (page 46), setting snaps (page 58), and sewing with waxed thread (page 54). The belt is a good project for tooling with a design. Review how to tool on page 61. Draw tooling samples on paper, or else experiment on your scrap leather, before you tackle the project itself.

Tools

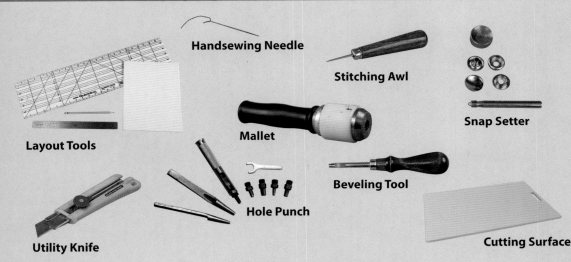

Handsewing Needle

Stitching Awl

Snap Setter

Layout Tools

Mallet

Beveling Tool

Utility Knife

Hole Punch

Cutting Surface

Leather Pattern: Belt with Buckle

Buckle end of belt

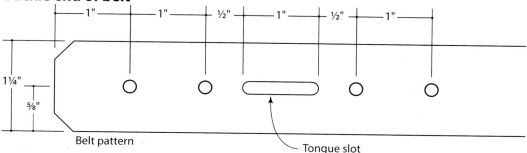

Belt pattern

Tongue slot

Loose end of belt

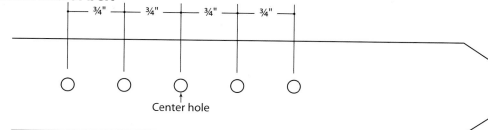

Center hole

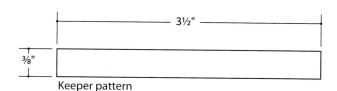

Keeper pattern

Leather
■ Vegetable-tanned leather, 7/8 oz. The width is 1¼" and the length is your waist size plus 8". Some leather suppliers sell belt blanks—you could get one of those if you don't want to cut your own. Start with a belt blank that is 48" long.

Supplies
■ #24 Snaps
■ Buckle
■ Thread
■ Wax
■ Dye (if you want to color your belt)

Skills
■ Measuring
■ Cutting
■ Punching holes
■ Sewing
■ Setting snaps
■ Beveling

Making: Belt with Buckle

1

Measure Your Waist
Feed the belt blank through the belt loops on your trousers and mark the distance around your waist. Add on 8". That is how long to cut your belt blank.

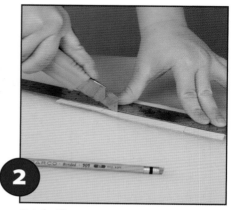

2

Cut the Keeper
After you cut the belt blank to the finished length, from the short extra length cut the small piece for the keeper, 3/8" wide x 3 1/2" long. To cut the little keeper you should tape the leather down to your cutting surface.

3

Transfer the Pattern
Mark the end of the belt that will have the buckle on it. Place the pattern alongside the belt blank and use the metal ruler and a pencil to transfer the markings to the leather.

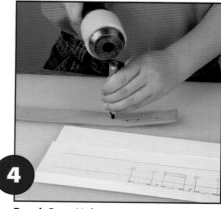

4

Punch Snap Holes
Punch the holes for the snaps and the ends of the slot that the buckle tongue will pass through. The holes at the other end of the belt, the ones you'll use to buckle your belt around your waist, will be punched later.

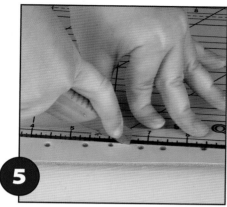

Cut the Tongue Slot

As the drawing shows, you need to connect two of the punched holes to make a slot for the buckle tongue. Carefully cut the slot using the utility knife and the clear, gridded ruler.

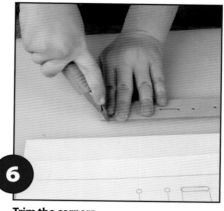

Trim the corners

Use the utility knife to trim the four corners off the ends of the belt. Trim a little deeper on the loose end, compared to the buckle end, as the pattern shows.

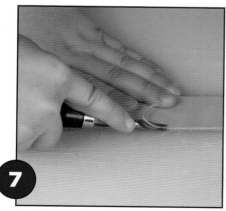

Bevel

Bevel all edges of the top surface of your belt. The belt leather is thick, making it easy to start the beveling tool. Remember to push the tool so it makes a little curl of leather.

Color the Belt

If you want to dye your belt, do that now. Be careful–the dye will color you too, so wear rubber gloves and an apron, and protect your work surface with a plastic grocery bag. Dye the keeper too!

Making: Belt with Buckle

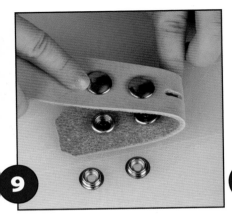

Set the Snaps
Stack the two pairs of snaps for holding the buckle and the belt keeper. Double check that they are stacked in order with the correct sides facing each other, and set the snaps (see page 58).

Punch Sewing Holes
Use the stitching awl to punch a small hole in each end of the keeper.

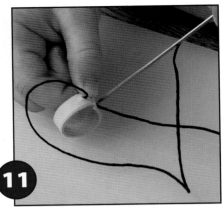

Stitch the Keeper
Now stitch the keeper together by angling your needle to get it into the holes. Stitch through the pair of holes several times, since you want this stitching to be strong.

Knot the Thread
Tie off your thread in a tight knot. The wax will help to hold the thread while you tie the knot. Trim the thread off but not too close to the knot just in case it does get a little loose.

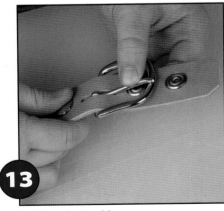

Position the Buckle
Position the buckle tongue in the slot with top side of the buckle on the top side of the belt. Fold the belt end over the buckle and close the first snap so it captures the buckle in the center of the fold.

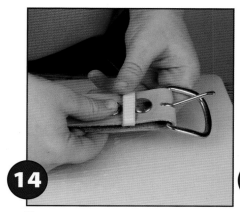

Keeper

Slide the keeper onto the belt so its stitching is on the back side. Slide it right up behind your first snap, and press the second snap closed to trap the keeper in place. Your belt is ready for its final fitting!

Mark Holes

To mark the belt holes wrap your belt around your waist, through the belt loops on your trousers. Make a pencil mark on the belt where it passes over the middle of the buckle's tongue. This will be your center hole.

Punch the Holes

Mark two holes on each side of your center hole. Space the holes ¾" apart. Punch all five holes using a punch that is just a bit larger than the buckle tongue.

Buckle your New Belt

Your belt is complete! Buckle your new belt around your waist. Doesn't that feel good?

Project

Camping Knife Pouch

This camping knife pouch fits tight to your belt horizontally instead of hanging down. This is better if you are hiking or camping because it won't get in your way as you are moving about. A snap fitting keeps the knife from falling out. At first the pouch will be very stiff and might not fit that well around your camping knife. As you use the pouch, keep it oiled and over time it will mold itself to the shape of your knife.

The project requires making a pattern (page 41), cutting the leather (page 43) and folding it, sewing a seam (page 54) and installing a snap (page 58). The pouch could be re-sized to fit your cell phone or any other small, rectangular object.

Tools

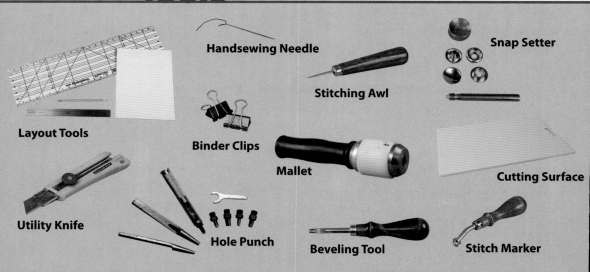

Layout Tools

Handsewing Needle

Stitching Awl

Snap Setter

Binder Clips

Mallet

Cutting Surface

Utility Knife

Hole Punch

Beveling Tool

Stitch Marker

Leather Pattern: Camping Knife Pouch

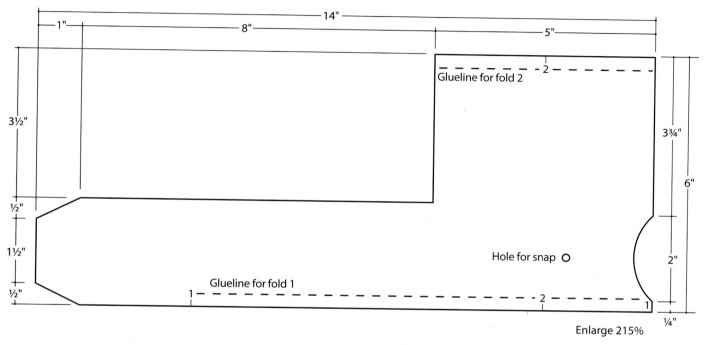

Glueline for fold 2

Glueline for fold 1

Hole for snap

Enlarge 215%

Leather
- 4/5 oz. vegetable-tanned leather, approx. 7" x 15"

Supplies
- Glue
- Thread
- Wax
- #24 Snap

Skills
- Measuring
- Cutting
- Punching holes
- Setting snaps
- Gluing
- Sewing

Making: Camping Knife Pouch

1

2

Oiling

To finish your camping knife pouch you need to oil it for a nice feel and soften the leather. Warming your vegetable oil in the microwave—just 15 seconds—helps the oil penetrate. Make sure the oil dries before using the camping knife pouch or it can cause stains. Dry it overnight or better yet, a few days.

Draw Pattern
Transfer the pattern to paper or use a copy machine to enlarge the pattern to the size you need. Trace the pattern onto the leather and cut it out. Be sure to accurately mark the numbers and fold lines on the leather. They show you where to make the folds and the order to fold them.

Punch Hole
Punch the hole for the bottom half of the snap. The hole for the top of the snap will be punched in the last step, so you can make the pouch flap fit just right.

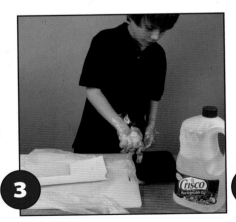

3

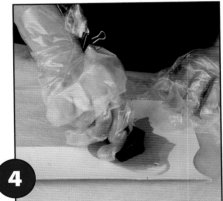

4

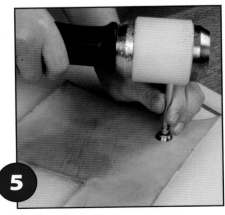

5

Apply Finish
Now is the time to oil the leather, and if you want to change its color, dye it before oiling.

Oil While Flat
It is easiest to apply finishing while the leather is still laying flat. After folding and sewing there are too many little corners to get the dye and oil into.

Set Snap Bottom
Set the bottom half of your snap. Place it so its opening is on the top side of the leather like in the photo.

First Fold
Case the leather with water (page 30), then fold the leather so number 1 meets number 1. Follow the folding instructions on page 111.

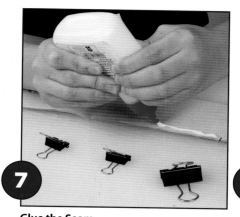

Glue the Seam
Spread white glue on the inside of the seam then press it tight together along the fold line.

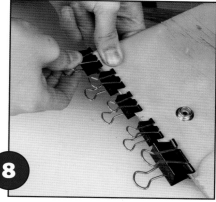

Clamp the Seam
Use binder clips to clamp the seam while the glue dries.

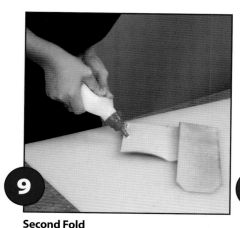

Second Fold
Apply glue and fold your leather so number 2 matches with number 2. It should fit neatly above the seam you just glued.

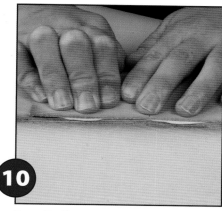

Press the Seam
Glue the new seam. Wipe off the excess glue, then let the glue firmly set.

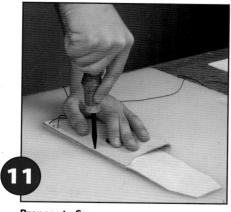

Prepare to Sew
Prepare to sew the seam by casing, marking and stabbing holes. The challenge is you are working three layers of leather. Hold the stitching awl straight up and down when stabbing the holes so you get a neat line of stitching on both sides. Then use the fid, as shown, to widen the holes.

Making: Camping Knife Pouch

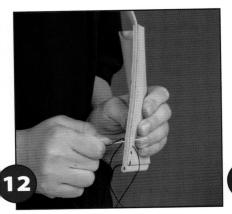

12

Sew Seam
Start at the top of the seam by the flap. Leave a 6" tail to sew in later. Do a running stitch the length of the leather, turn and stitch back up (see page 54). It is tough to push the needle through three layers of leather. If the punched holes are tight, enlarge them with the fid.

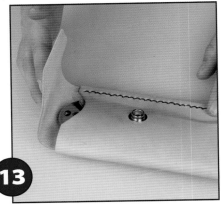

13

Mark Snap
Put your knife in the pouch. Fold the flap over so you have a tight fit. Can you feel the snap underneath?

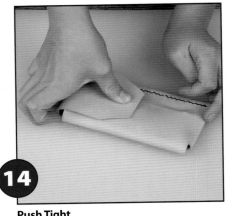

14

Push Tight
Push down so it makes a mark inside the flap. This is where to punch the hole for the top part of the snap.

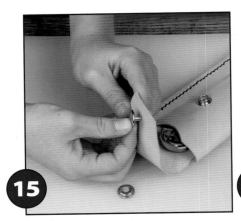

15

Punch
Punch the hole centered on your mark. Assemble the snap top in the hole. Don't set it yet! Double check you have it just right first.

16

Set
Now set the snap with the anvil, setter, and mallet. Try the pouch on your belt. See how closely it fits to your body?

Bonus Project: Make Mine a Wrist Band

It's easy to convert your bookmark project (page 62) into a wristband. The pattern is the same and the leather is the same size.

Just add a snap at each end following the instructions on page 58. You might like to decorate the wrist band with your name or initials by punching holes in the leather (page 46) or tooling it (page 61).

Place the Anvil
Place the anvil with the concave side up. Place your eyelet on the anvil, post side up. Fit the punched hole in your leather over the eyelet post. Add the stud with the flat side down. It will slip right on the eyelet post and slide down onto the leather. Follow the remaining instructions on page 58.

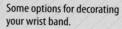
The completed wrist band.

Some options for decorating your wrist band.

Project

Keepsake Box

This box has a slide-off lid and can be used to keep all kinds of things. The box can be simple or decorated. The one shown has been dyed green. The project makes a wonderful gift, by itself or as the box with a special gift inside. Once you learn the basic construction you can build boxes of many different shapes and sizes.

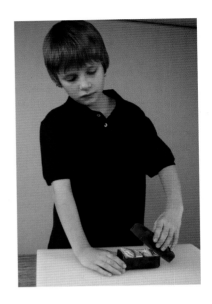

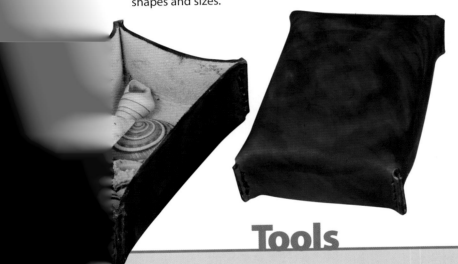

Tools

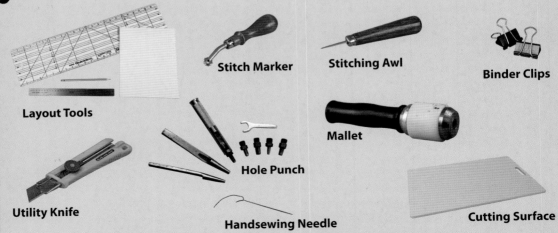

Layout Tools

Stitch Marker

Stitching Awl

Binder Clips

Utility Knife

Hole Punch

Mallet

Handsewing Needle

Cutting Surface

Leather Pattern: Keepsake Box

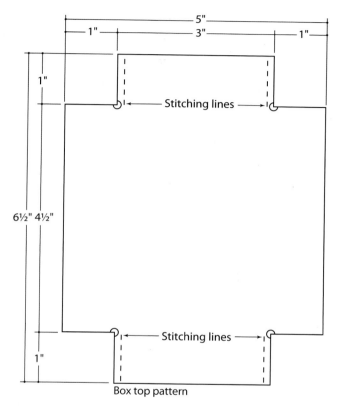

Box top pattern

Enlarge 185%

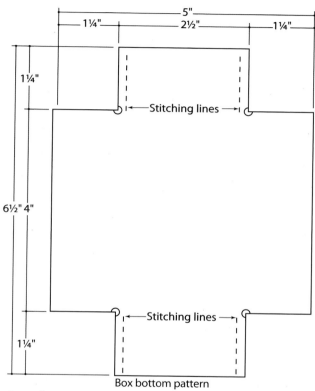

Box bottom pattern

Leather
- 4/5 oz. vegetable-tanned leather, approx. 6" x 7" and 5½" x 7"

Supplies
- Glue
- Thread
- Wax

Skills
- Measuring
- Punching holes
- Cutting
- Gluing
- Sewing

Making: Keepsake Box

Dye the Leather
If you want to dye the leather for the box, do it before you cut it to the pattern. You could also color the leather with markers, or stamp a pattern on it.

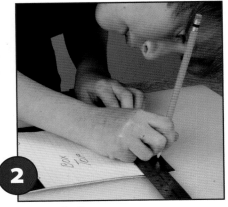

Lay Out the Pattern
Transfer the measurements from the drawing onto a piece of paper and cut it out. Trace it onto the leather.

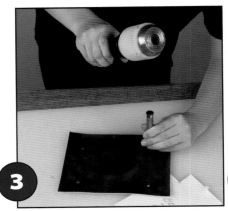

Punch The Holes
Place the leather on a cutting surface and punch the corner holes. The round corners will make it easier to fold the box sides to make the corners.

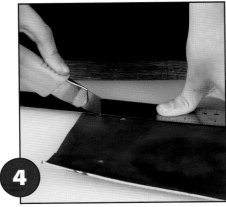

Cut the Leather
Cut out the corners next, starting with your knife point at the center of the circles. Finish cutting the sides.

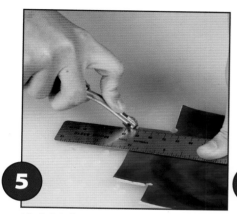

5

Mark Stitching Lines
Mark the stitching lines from the drawing. Lightly case these edges and use the stitching wheel to mark the sewing holes (see page 53).

6

Glue Corners
Apply the glue onto the edges of the corners. Line up the edges and clamp with the binder clips.

7

Let Glue Set
Let the glue set for 15 minutes. Use the time to clean off the table, wax the thread, and thread the needle.

8

Punch Sewing Holes
Use your stitching awl, as described on page 48, to pierce the sewing holes. This can be tricky—keep the leather flat on the work surface so you don't pierce your fingertips!

9

Sew The Corners
Start at the top edge of the corner. Leave a 6" tail of thread. Sew a running stitch to the end of the holes, turn, and stitch back to the top edge. See how stitching back has filled all the spaces? This makes a strong seam.

10

Backstitching
Now stitch back into the last three holes and remove the needle. Rethread your needle with the 6" tail thread, backstitch, then trim both threads. Do all of the corners the same way.

Drawstring Bag for Game Boy

This sturdy drawstring bag can have many uses. You can use it to carry things or save collections. The bag shown is a good fit for a pocket game boy or a portable CD player. What else can you think of for a drawstring bag like this?

Tools

Screw Eye Needle

Utility Knife

Layout Tools

Binder Clips

Hole Punch

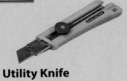

Mallet

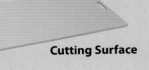

Cutting Surface

Leather Pattern: Drawstring Bag for Game Boy

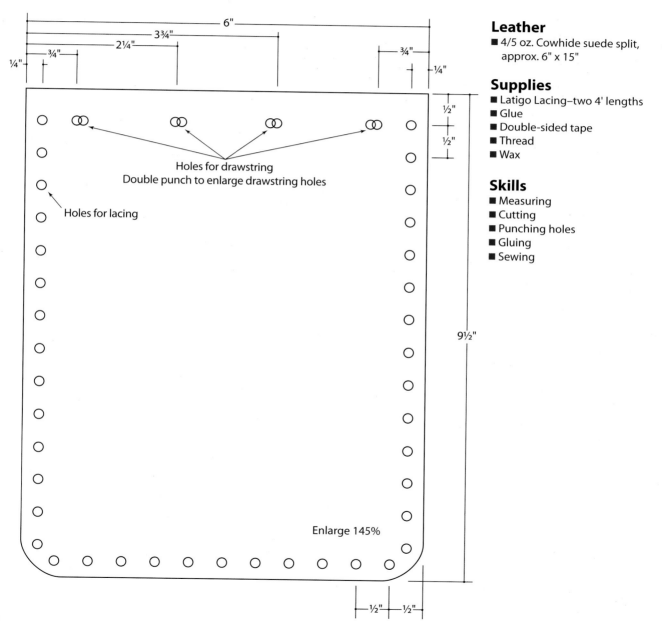

Holes for drawstring
Double punch to enlarge drawstring holes

Holes for lacing

Enlarge 145%

Leather
- 4/5 oz. Cowhide suede split, approx. 6" x 15"

Supplies
- Latigo Lacing–two 4' lengths
- Glue
- Double-sided tape
- Thread
- Wax

Skills
- Measuring
- Cutting
- Punching holes
- Gluing
- Sewing

Making: Drawstring Bag for Game Boy

Lay Out the Pattern
Transfer the measurements from the drawing onto a piece of paper and cut it out. The dimensions fit a game, toy, or a CD player. You can enlarge or reduce the pattern to fit something else.

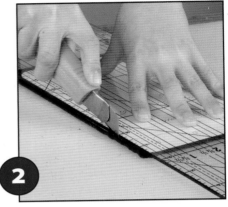

Cut the Leather
Use double-sided tape to attach the pattern onto the suede. Later when you remove the tape, some of the suede fuzzy will come off but that is fine. Cut the suede around the pattern. Leave the pattern on the leather.

Glue Sides
Place suede taped with the pattern on top of the remaining suede, with the best-looking sides to the outside. Glue the three edges that will be laced together. Weigh them down with a stack of old magazines for 15 minutes while the glue sets.

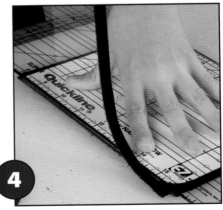

Trim the Leather
When the glue has dried, use the clear, gridded ruler and the utility knife to trim the second piece of leather to the exact same size as the one with the pattern on it.

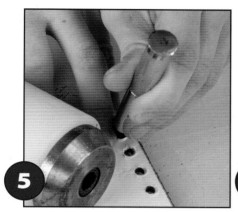

Punch the Holes

Use the hole punch and mallet to punch right through the pattern and the two layers of suede at the same time. After the holes are punched, peel the pattern off.

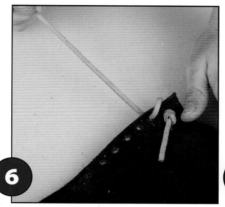

Lace the Leather

Thread the screw eye needle onto the lacing, make a knot, and start sewing at one corner.

Knot Free End

Sew using a whip stitch all the way around the bag, then knot the free end of the lace and cut it off.

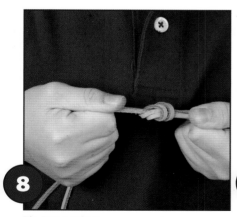

Tie Drawstring

Cut two 18" length of leather lacing, double them, and tie an overhand knot near the folded place in each, to form a loop with two long tails.

Install Drawstring

Thread the long tails through the two outside holes at the top of the bag, so the loop is on the outside and the tails are on the inside.

Making: Drawstring Bag for Game Boy

10

Knot the Drawstring
The two long tails in a square knot on the inside of the bag, as shown. This anchors the drawstring.

11

Tie the Free Ends
Following the photo, lace the drawstring through the top holes and tie the free ends together. Repeat with the other length of lacing, from the other side of the bag.

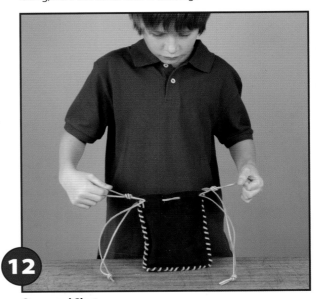

12

Open and Shut
Pulling one set of loops closes the bag, pulling the other set opens it.

Project

Moccasins

Moccasins are the all-around handy shoe. They are soft enough to wear indoors as a slipper, and strong enough for occasional outdoor wear. You can make them in cowhide split suede, which is available in many colors. The pattern given here is for both the right and the left moccasin. It can sized on a copy machine to fit your feet. You can make moccasins for your whole family!

Tools

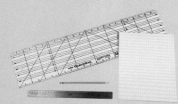

Layout Tools

Screw-eye Needle

Mallet

Utility Knife

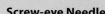

Hole Punch

Cutting Surface

Leather Pattern: Moccasins

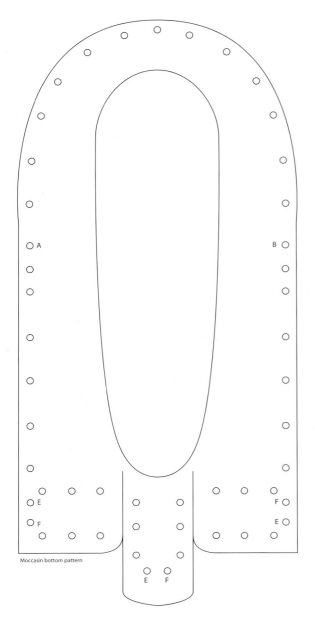

Moccasin bottom pattern

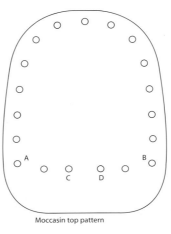

Moccasin top pattern

Leather
- Cowhide suede split–4/5 oz., a piece big enough for two patterns–remember, you have two feet!

Supplies
- Lacing–7 yards of latigo lace
- Glue
- Double-sided tape

Skills
- Measuring
- Cutting
- Punching holes
- Gluing
- Lacing

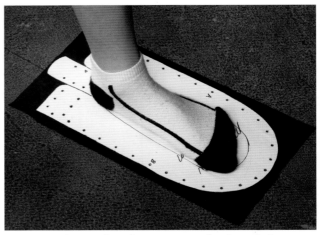

Use a copy machine to enlarge this pattern so your foot fits inside the center shape. Make two copies–one for each foot.

Making: Moccasins

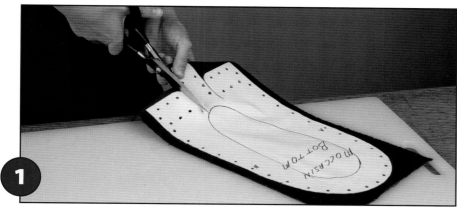

Cut Pattern Parts
Check that the pattern fits your foot, then use double-sided tape to fasten it onto the suede. Cut out the shape, but leave the pattern taped on. Tape the second pattern to the other piece of suede.

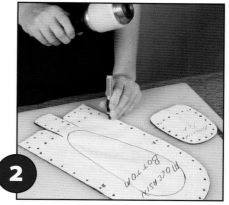

Punch Holes
Use the mallet and hole punch to make the holes. Punch right through the pattern and the suede together. When you are finished punching, you can remove the pattern.

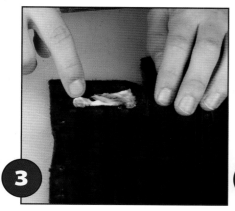

Glue Heel
Spread glue on the overlapping heel sections. Suede absorbs glue so be sure you have enough on it.

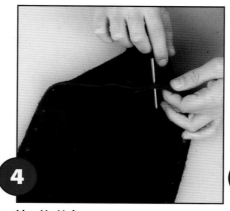

Line Up Holes
Use the lacing needle to help line up the holes E and F, and the remaining heel holes.

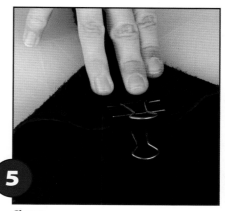

Clamp
Clamp the glued seam with binder clips.

Making: Moccasins

Locate the Top
The holes on the toe top are spaced closer together than the holes on the shoe bottom. This is so the bottom gathers up to form the moccasin sides. Place the toe top on the bottom and line up holes A and B.

Knot the Lace
Load the screw-eye lacing needle (page 28) with the lace cut four times longer than the seam and tie a knot at the end of the threaded lace. A single overhand knot will be enough.

Sew the Top
Start at the hole marked A on the pattern, and whip-stitch around the toe to hole B.

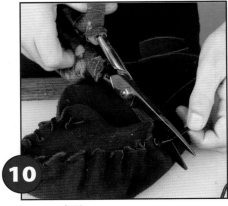

Gather the Stitching
See how the bottom gathers as you match up the holes and sew. Keep the top piece as flat as you can while the bottom gathers.

Knot and Trim
Pull the lace snug. Tie a knot and trim off the extra lace.

Lace the Heel
Lace the heel as shown and tie off the top in a knot or bow.

Lace Sides
Start at hole C and leave a 12" tail to use as the shoe tie. Sew a running stitch across the top to the closest edge, around the sides of the shoe, and then up across the top. The lace should emerge at hole D. Cut off the lace 12" from the shoe. This is your other shoe tie.

Tie the Laces
Put your moccasin on and tie it up. Very nice. Now make another moccasin for the other foot!

Project

Book Cover

Some books—your journal or diary, for example, an important school book, your mother's checkbook, or your big three-ring binder—need the protection of a custom-fitted leather cover. You can decorate a leather book cover any way you like, by stamping and tooling the leather, by dyeing it, or by adding a bold stripe with a colored permanent marker, as shown here.

The book cover has a large surface so here is a project where you could select a leather piece with the beauty marks of fat wrinkles or a ranch brand. These markings could add an interesting look to your project.

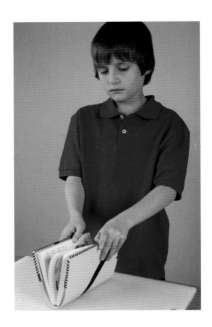

Tools

Layout Tools

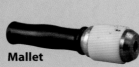

Mallet

Lok-eye Lacing Needle

Utility Knife

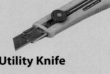

Hole Punch

Lacing Chisels— single- and four-prong

Cutting Surface

Leather Pattern: Book Cover

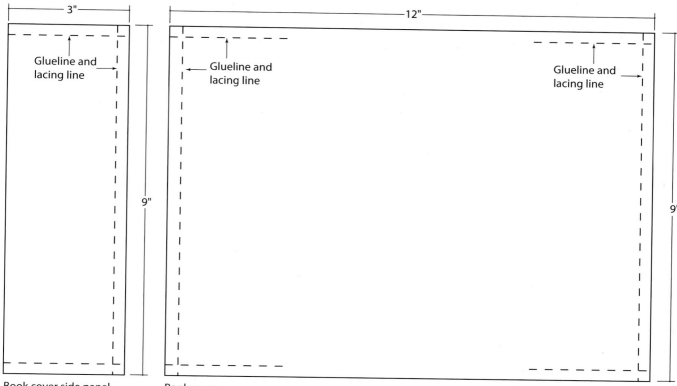

3"

12"

Glueline and lacing line

Glueline and lacing line

Glueline and lacing line

9"

9"

Book cover side panel
Cut 2 3" x 9"
■ for 5" x 8" book

Book cover
9" x 12"
■ for 5" x 8" book

Leather
■ 2/3 oz. vegetable-tanned cowhide, about 10" x 13" and 6" x 10"

Supplies
■ Glue
■ Lacing–7' of plastic lacing or $1/8$" leather lacing

Skills
■ Measuring
■ Cutting
■ Gluing
■ Punching holes
■ Lacing

Making: Book Cover

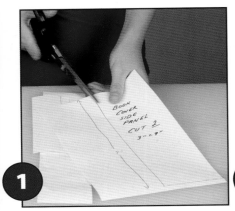

1

Cut the Pattern
Use the gridded ruler to draw the pattern. The grid will help you draw straight lines and make sharp corners. Cut out the pattern pieces and transfer them to the leather.

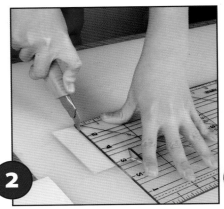

2

Cut the Leather
Use the ruler to guide your knife along the lines. Remember where you have placed all your fingers!

3

Add Color
Use permanent markers to draw a design or perhaps print your name onto the book cover. It's best to work out the design on paper first, so you know how the design will fit or how large to print.

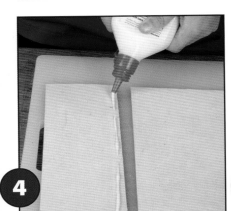

4

Glue Edges
Spread the glue, then put the parts together. Wipe off any extra glue with a damp cloth.

5

Align Edges
Be sure to line up the edges while the glue is still wet.

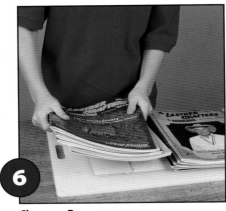

6

Clamp or Press
Clamp the glued seam with binder clips, or press it under a stack of heavy magazines.

Making the Book Cover

Place your book cover on the cutting surface, and trim off the points of the corners. Use the fid to make a layout line, then punch the corner lacing holes using the single-hole chisel (page 48).

Punch Lacing Holes

Now use the four-prong chisel to make lacing holes on the three glued edges of the cover flaps. Look at page 49 to review how to space the holes on the edges.

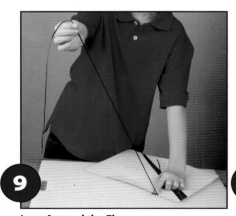

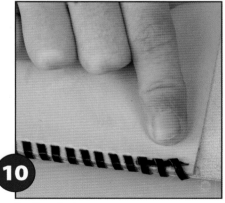

Lace Around the Flap

Lace around the flap; see page 27 for threading the lok-eye needle and making the whip stitch. Lacing looks great when it is all neat and not twisted. Prevent twists by running the lace between your fingers.

Ending the Lace

When you finish lacing, end off by running the free end under three stitches, pull the stitches tight, and cut the lace off close to the leather.

Making: Book Cover

Ooops!

Sometimes the lacing chisel slips off the line and you get a row of holes in the wrong place (right) . You could start over with another piece of leather, but usually you don't need to do that. Just make a new row of holes where they are supposed to be, and continue with the project. The lacing will cover the extra holes.

Sometimes, despite your best efforts, flat lacing gets twisted (below left). Usually you can fix it by twisting the lace with needle-nose pliers. Grab the lace close to the leather and twist. Sometimes you have to undo the stitch and re-lace it (below right).

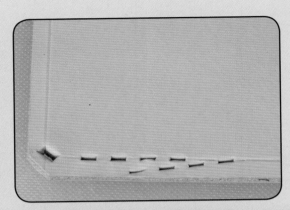

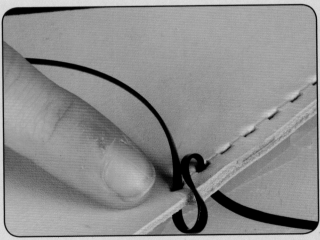

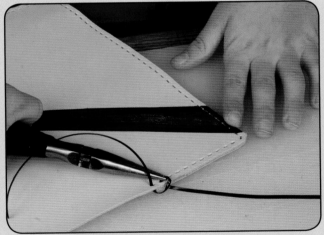

Project

Cell Phone Case

This belt carrier has been designed to fit a regular cell phone, but is easy to modify it to fit many other things you might want to carry on your belt. You could make it big enough for an iPod or a Game Boy, and if you made it of heavier leather, it could hold your Dad's tape measure. The phone case shown in the photo is fastened together with rivets, while the tape measure case has eyelets.

Tools

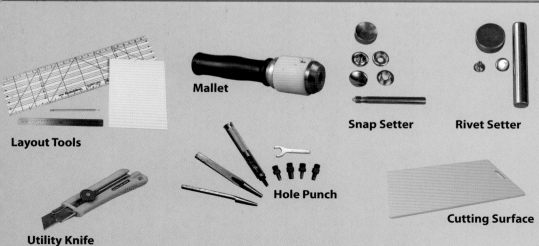

Layout Tools

Mallet

Snap Setter

Rivet Setter

Utility Knife

Hole Punch

Cutting Surface

Leather Pattern: Cell Phone Case

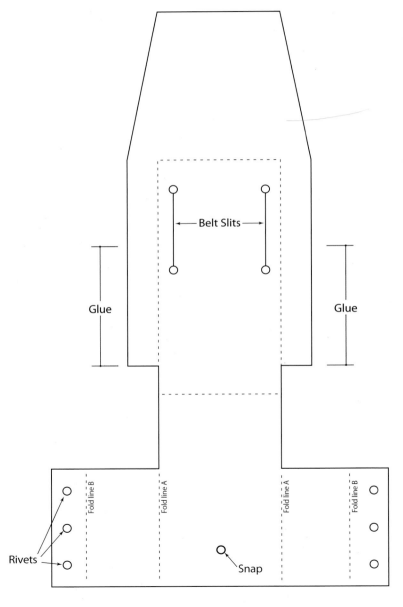

Belt Slits

Glue

Glue

Fold line B

Fold line A

Fold line A

Fold line B

Rivets

Snap

Leather
- 4/5 oz. vegetable-tanned cowhide, about 8" x 10"

Supplies
- Glue
- #24 Snap
- Rivets
- Dye

Skills
- Measuring
- Punching holes
- Cutting
- Folding
- Gluing
- Setting rivets and snaps

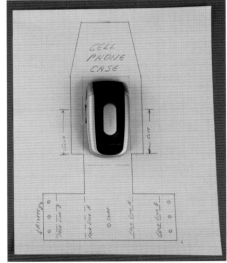

Adjust the pattern so the object you want to carry fits inside the center rectangle with an extra 1/4" all around.

Making: Cell Phone Case

Draw the Pattern
Draw your pattern on paper from the leather layout. Cut out the paper pattern and fold it to check the fit with your cell phone. Adjust the pattern to fit, or make a new one.

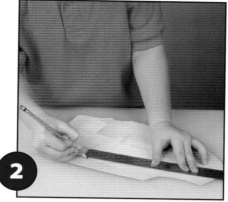

Transfer Pattern
Tape the pattern onto the leather and trace around it. This pattern is an odd shape and you might find it fits easily within a piece of scrap leather.

Punch Holes
Punch the rivet holes, the holes for the belt slits, and the hole for the bottom of the snap.

Cut Leather
Cut out the outline of the carrier and the slits for your belt. Use the metal ruler and a sharp utility knife.

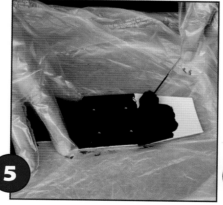

Color
If you want to dye the case, now is the time to do that. Dye both sides and all the edges. Also oil the leather so it will bend easily. If you want to put a top finish on, you can do that, too, after the oil is very dry.

Set Snap Bottom
Set the snap with its open side on the top of the leather. Double check its position before you set it with the anvil, setter, and mallet.

Making: Cell Phone Case

7

Fold
Make folds at lines A and B. On line A, fold the flesh sides together. On line B, fold the smooth sides together. You can review how to make crisp folds on page 111 of the wallet project.

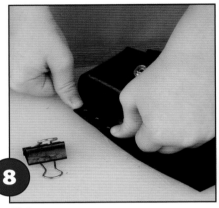

8

Gluing
The leather layout drawing shows where to glue the seams. Before gluing the case, fold it to check how it goes together. Now line up the edges, spread the glue, and clamp with the binder clips.

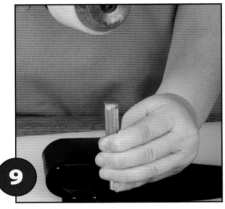

9

Punch Holes
After the glue has set, punch the rivet holes in the glued flaps through both thicknesses. Remember to hold the punch as straight up and down as you can!

10

Set the Rivets
Set the three rivets on either side of the base, using the rivet setter and anvil.

11

Locate the Snap Cap
Before you can install the snap, you have to figure out exactly where it should be. Put your phone in the case and fold the flap over. Feel the snap bottom through the leather and push gently (your phone is inside) to make a mark.

12

Set the Snap Cap
Remove your phone. Punch the hole, set the snap, and there you are!

Bonus Project: Tape Measure Case

Modifying the belt case pattern to accommodate other objects is relatively simple. Once you've determined the correct sizing, follow the same steps as the belt case project.

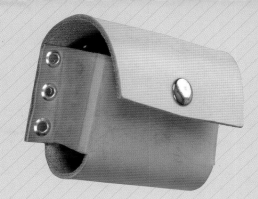

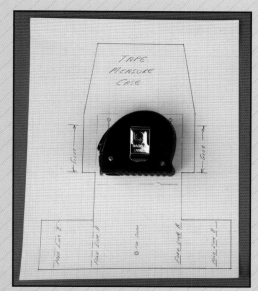

Adjust the Pattern
Adjust the pattern so the object you want to carry fits inside the center rectangle with an extra 1/4" all around.

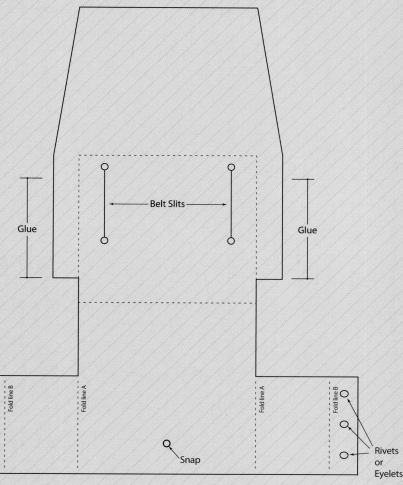

Belt Slits

Glue

Glue

Fold line B

Fold line A

Fold line A

Fold line B

Rivets
or
Eyelets

Snap

Rivets
or
Eyelets

Project

Wallet

This wallet is magically made. No sewing, just cut and fold, fold, fold, and then a dab of glue and fold some more. It's the most complex pattern in this book. The challenge is in the precise cutting of the leather, and thinner leather will be easier too. Copy and enlarge the pattern to make a full-size pattern. You might want to make a few copies on which to draw your tooling or color marker ideas.

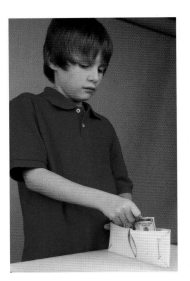

The simple stamping pattern shown here is just to get you started. You can develop any design you like, working on paper and scrap leather before you stamp the project itself. Stamp while the leather is flat, before you fold it into a wallet.

Tools

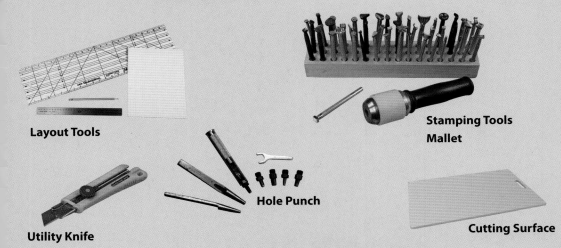

Layout Tools

Utility Knife

Hole Punch

Stamping Tools
Mallet

Cutting Surface

Leather Pattern: Wallet

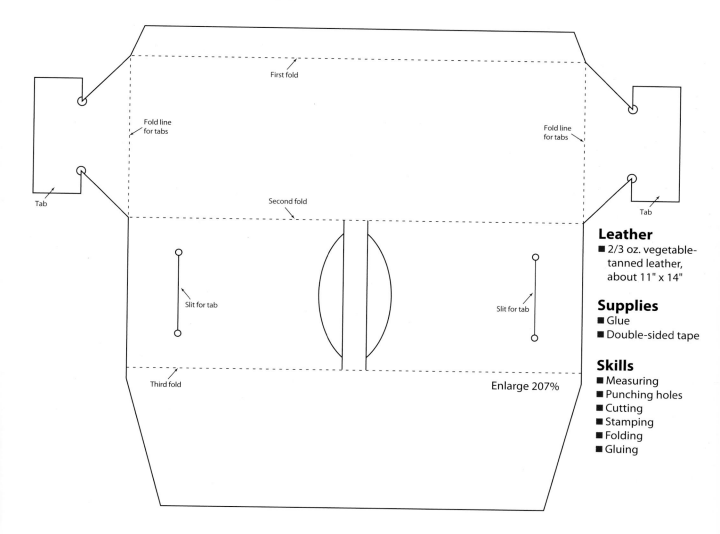

First fold

Fold line for tabs

Fold line for tabs

Tab

Second fold

Tab

Slit for tab

Slit for tab

Third fold

Enlarge 207%

Leather
- 2/3 oz. vegetable-tanned leather, about 11" x 14"

Supplies
- Glue
- Double-sided tape

Skills
- Measuring
- Punching holes
- Cutting
- Stamping
- Folding
- Gluing

Making: Wallet

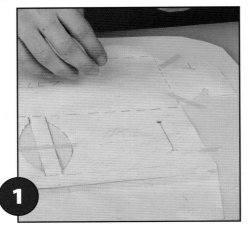

1

Pattern Layout
Choose where on the leather you want to place your pattern. Now turn it over so that the flesh side, which will be the inside, is facing up. Tape the pattern to this side of the leather.

2

Punch Holes
Punch holes as shown on the drawing. Now cut the slit between the holes. The holes in the tabs will lock into the holes at the ends of the slits.

3

Cut Pattern
Cut the pattern using the metal ruler to guide your cutter. Place your ruler on the pattern side of the lines then; if you slip, you will cut into the scrap leather and not into the project.

4

Mark Fold Lines
Remove the pattern and use a pencil to mark the fold lines on the flesh side of the leather. If you want to dye the leather or put some other finish on it, or stamp or tool it, now is the time.

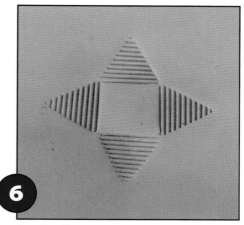

Stamp a Pattern
Prepare the leather by casing the front side with water. Avoid a stain by casing all of it. Then stamp your design.

Just One Stamp
This simple example shows what you can do with a single stamp.

Skills: Folding Practice

Practice this technique before doing it on your wallet! Very lightly case the pencil line for the fold on the flesh side. Dampen it just a little bit, because too much water will stain.

Place the metal ruler alongside the pencil line and fold up against it. Remove the ruler and push the folded leather all the way over and down.

Tap the fold with your mallet to get it as flat as possible.

Making: Wallet

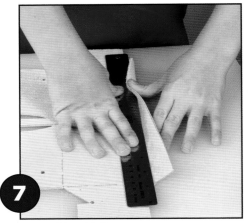

First Fold on Wallet

The first line to fold is the long narrow flap at the top of the pattern. Do it how you learned in the folding practice, using the metal ruler and tapping the fold to flatten it.

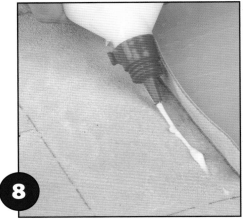

Glue the Flap

This little flap is glued. Brush glue under the flap and weigh it down or clamp it with binder clips.

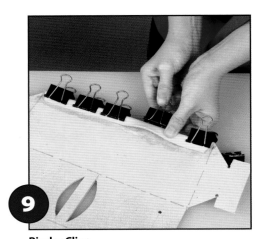

Binder Clips

Be careful! If your leather is damp from folding, the clips may leave marks.

Second and Third Folds

Case the flesh side and fold the other two long lines. Tap the folds down flat, but don't glue them.

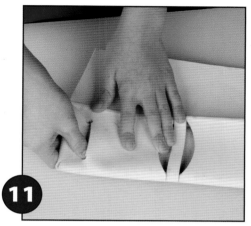

End Folds

Open up the folds so the leather lays flat again. Case and fold the end flaps in. Refold the long side and tuck the tabs into the slot so the punched holes interlock.

Last Fold

You already made the last long fold; now tuck it into the wallet so it lines the inside.

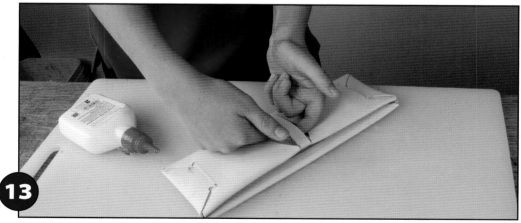

A Dab of Glue

Smear a bit of glue under the center bar and press it down tight. This part helps hold the wallet together, and makes a ridge so things don't easily slide out of the pockets.

Project

Hatchet Holster

This hatchet holster is handy because it hangs on your belt, keeping the tool ready to use. It also protects the cutting edge of the hatchet. This project uses all of the skills you have learned in this book.

The hatchet holster can be colored in any way you like. The top finish needs to be weatherproof and waterproof so you can take it outside.

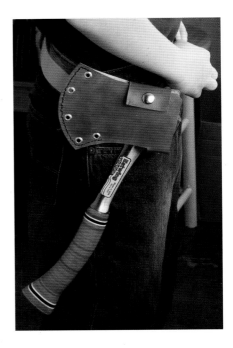

Tools

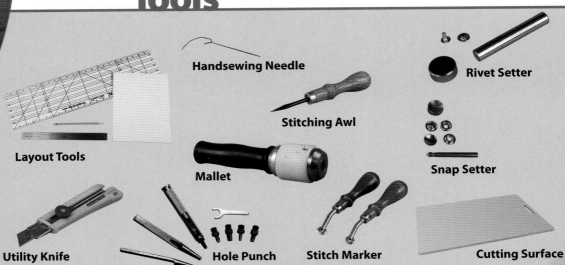

Handsewing Needle

Stitching Awl

Rivet Setter

Layout Tools

Mallet

Snap Setter

Utility Knife

Hole Punch

Stitch Marker

Cutting Surface

Leather Pattern: Hatchet Holster

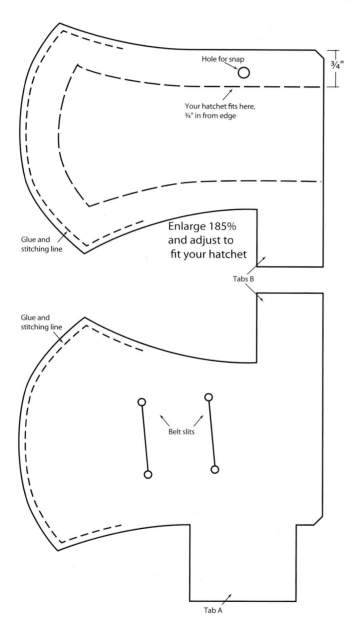

Hole for snap

Your hatchet fits here, ¾" in from edge

¾"

Glue and stitching line

Enlarge 185% and adjust to fit your hatchet

Tabs B

Glue and stitching line

Belt slits

Tab A

Leather
- 4/5 oz. vegetable-tanned leather, about 9" x 11"

Supplies
- Thread
- Wax
- Rivets or eyelets
- #24 Snaps
- Glue

Skills
- Measuring
- Cutting
- Punching holes
- Setting rivets
- Setting snaps
- Gluing
- Sewing
- Dyeing
- Oiling and finishing

Making: Hatchet Holster

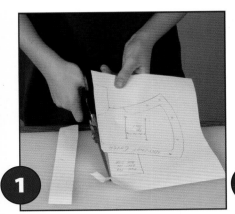

1

Adjust the Pattern
Use a copy machine to enlarge the pattern. Compare it to your hatchet. You might need to adjust the pattern to fit your hatchet. The holster should be 3/4" bigger than your hatchet on the top, front and bottom edges. The back can be the same. Cut the pattern out.

2

Punch the Holes
Tape your pattern onto the leather. Punch the holes for the belt slits on the side with Tab A. Also punch the hole for the snap bottom on the side without Tab A. Don't punch the holes for the rivets on the front edges of the holster. Wait until after you have completed the stitching.

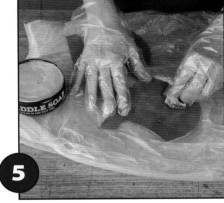

3

Cut the Leather
Cut the leather along the pattern outlines. Use the utility knife and the metal ruler. The trick is to cut smooth curves and straight lines.

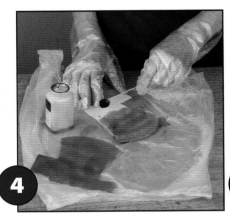

4

Dye the Leather
If you want to color the leather, do it now, before assembling the pieces (see page 33 for more on dyeing).

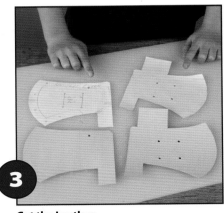

5

Waterproofing
When the dye has dried, protect the leather with a waterproof finish.

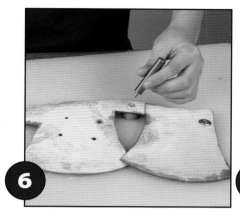

Set Snap Bottom

Overlap and glue tabs B. When the glue has set, punch a hole through both pieces and set a rivet or eyelet in the hole. Use your snap anvil, setter, and mallet to set the snap bottom with its open side on the top of the leather.

Glue the Front

Glue the front edges as marked on the pattern and clamp it with binder clips. While the glue is setting, clean the worktable and prepare for sewing by waxing your thread and threading your needle.

Stitching

Case the leather and mark the stitching line. Use the stitching awl to make the stitching holes around the curved end of the leather, then use a running stitch to sew the seam. For the details of sewing see page 54.

Punch Rivet Holes

Make marks for the five reinforcing rivets or eyelets. They should be behind the stitching so you don't cut through the thread of the seam. When you are pleased with their placement, punch the holes and set the fasteners.

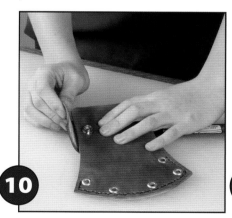

Locate the Snap Cap

Put your hatchet inside the holster. Fold Tab A over the bottom of the snap and pull it snug around your hatchet. Push down on the tab so the snap bottom marks it.

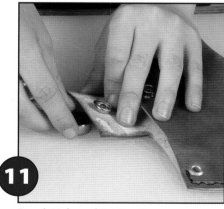

Punch Hole and Set Top Snap

To finish the holster, punch the snap hole where you marked it and set the snap top.

Glossary

This glossary has some terms you will find in the book's text and are listed again here for speedy reference. There are also new terms you might read or hear when learning more about leather.

Aging: A leather's ability to retain its original character over time. The usual problem is the leather becomes brittle or the color changes.

Bovine: An animal belonging to the ox or cow family.

Carving: Another word for tooling, the process of using hand tools on cased vegetable-tanned leather to make impressed patterns.

Casing: Dampening vegetable-tanned tooling leather so it will soften to be tooled and molded.

Chrome tanning: Leather tanning process with chromium salts to make soft, mellow hides that are easily dyed at the tannery.

Cowhide: Term applied to leather made from the hide of cows, but the word sometimes means any leather tanned from bovine animals

Embossed leather: Leather that has a pattern made under high pressure in a press. This is to create a design, or to make a hide appear to be another leather, such as embossing an ostrich pattern into cowhide.

Fat wrinkle: Wrinkles in the grain of leather caused by fat deposits in the animal, they create part of the beauty in leather.

Finish: All processes done to leather after it has been tanned are called finishes. We finish leather to enhance it, for example by coloring, creating a special texture or pattern, or waterproofing.

Flesh side: The inner of a hide.

Grain: The outside of the hide or skin showing the pores, cells, wrinkles and other characteristics that make up the natural texture of the leather.

Hair-on hide: Leather that has been tanned with the hair left on. This includes sheep shearling, and hair-on cowhides.

Hide: The pelt of a animal.

Leather: An animal hide which has been preserved and processed by tanning.

Leatherette: A manmade product that imitates leather.

Light fastness: The resistance of a leather to change color when exposed to sunlight. Leather can become darker (just as we tan in sunlight) or become faded.

Liming: The wet process that removes the hair of the animal, preparing it for tanning.

Matte finish: A flat or dull finish.

Natural markings: Variations on the leather surface including wrinkles, scratches, brands, and color changes.

Nubuck: A brushed, grain-sueded leather. This suede leather is often used in shoes because of its durability.

Patent leather: Leather with a glossy waterproof finish produced by coats of oils, varnish, or resins.

Patina: A natural wearing that develops on leather over time through normal use, giving it a mellow look.

Pelt: The skin of a fur bearing animal when removed from the carcass.

Rawhide: Untanned or partially tanned cattle hides.

Shearling: A sheepskin with the wool hair left on.

Side leather: Full hides that have been cut in half along the backbone or bend to make two sides.

Split leather: Leather made from the bottom split of the hide, usually cowhide.

Splitting: Cutting leather into two or more layers before tanning.

Stamping: Using hand tools on cased vegetable-tanned leather to make impressed patterns.

Suede: Leather that has a velvety nap.

Sueding: The process of raising fibers on a hide or skin to create a velvet nap.

Tanning: The process of making raw hides into leather.

Top grain: The top outer layer of a hide.

Top coat: A transparent finish applied to the leather surface.

Upholstery leather: A term for leather processed for many uses, including furniture, car seats, or airplane seats.

Vegetable or bark tanning: The tanning process that uses the tannic acid from tree bark, leaves, and nuts. The process leaves the leather dry and flexible but when dampened can be molded and tooled.

Weight: The weight of leather is how the thickness of a leather is marked. It is measured in ounces per square foot. Each ounce of leather weight equals $\frac{1}{64}$" in thickness.

Resources

To guide you further on your journey of learning about leatherworking, here are more places to look for information. Some of the books can be found at your public library. Because they are such specialized books, your library might not have them but can get them through an interlibrary loan.

Ask your librarian about this.

Books

Evans, Timothy H. *King of the Western Saddle*. University Press of Mississippi, 1998

Hutchins, Dan and Sebie. *Old Cowboy Saddles & Spurs*. Sante Fe, NM: Hutchins Publishing Co., 1996

Price, Byron B. *Fine Art of the West*. Abbeville Press, 2004

Stohlman, Al. *The Art of Making Leather Cases*. Fort Worth, Texas: Tandy Leather Co., 1979

Stohlman, Al, A. D. Patten, and J. A. Wilson. *Leatherwork Manual*. Fort Worth, Texas: Tandy Leather Co., 1969

Magazines

The Leather Crafters & Saddlers Journal, published in Rhinelander, Wis., is the only American magazine that deals only with leather working. It is filled with projects, history, leather and tool resources, and information on leather working workshops, guilds and exhibits.

Web Sites

There are many Web sites about leather and leather working. Searching the Web for different sites is a project to do with an adult. Some of the sites listed here are for tool and leather suppliers, sites that have lots of information.

Suppliers

www.hidehouse.com   www.leathersupply.com
www.tandyleather.com   www.csosborne.com

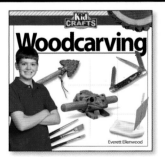